CREATURE
TEACHERS

YEHWEHNODE
GRANDMOTHER TWYLAH NITSCH

· · · · · · · · · · · · ·

CREATURE
TEACHERS

· · · · · · · · · · · · ·

A Guide to
the Spirit Animals
of the Native
American Tradition

CONTINUUM · NEW YORK

1998
The Continuum Publishing Company
370 Lexington Avenue
New York, NY 10017

Printed in the United States of America

Library of Congress Cataloging-in-Publication Data
Nitsch, Twylah Hurd.
Creature teachers : a guide to the spirit animals of the Native
American Tradition / Yehwehnode (Twylah Nitsch).
    p. cm.
ISBN 0-8264-1023-5
1. Seneca Indians—Folklore.   2. Animals—Folklore.
3. Teaching—Aids and devices.   I. Title.
E99.S3N56 1997
398.24'5'08997—dc20   96-45038
                                    CIP

INTRODUCTION

Moses and Alice Shongo were my first teachers, counselors, and caretakers. They were my Elders, the Grandfather, and the Grandmother, who helped me honor my Creature Teachers.

I feel exceedingly fortunate to have been raised in the Native Way of wholeness; knowing all creatures are our family and relatives. Creature Teachers reflects the qualities of the earth connection; we need to expand our awareness through these lessons, to achieve a life of being fulfilled. The qualities, characterized by these creatures are placed on a **Wisdom Wheel, the Symbol of Wholeness.**

This book has been written to share the wonderful way of life that is expressed by these Creature Teachers. Nature is their school. Nature is our school. Let's look through Nature's eyes and accept the beauty within our reach and learn how to grow through our knowingness.

Dedication

Creature Teachers is dedicated to the people who volunteered their time, energy, and love to make their dream become a reality: Jessica, Beth, Wata, Kitty, Samantha, Felicity, Ron, Kate, Carol, Helen, Mary Jane, Alix, Shaun, Bob, and Jim, in addition to the Intensives who shared its wisdom.

Life abundant quickens us Now
Love Eternal, tells us how.

Twylah Nitsch

HOW TO USE CREATURE TEACHERS: THE FORMAT

1. There is only one philosophy used in Creature Teachers and this is honesty.

2. We tap into this honesty through intuition.

3. Intuition is the perfect law within.

4. We accept intuition as lessons we learned in former life experiences.

5. Intuition is alive.

6. It is energized through truth.

7. This truth is centered within our nature and ever present.

8. There are no options for Creature Teachers. However, humankind selects options when they are not connected to their truth within.

9. To be connected takes diligent practice and serves stability as the purpose.

10. Creature Teachers have this stability and have maintained and lived it from the beginning of time.

11. A bear is a bear, a wolf a wolf without denial. The intuitive energy is manifested when the Creature Teachers are selected by an individual.

12. There are 52 circles, of which each circle signifies a Creature Teacher. Five plus two equals seven. Seven symbolizes the Pathway of Peace. The number eight represents love and the number nine represents Peace.

13. The moment we randomly select 9 circles form the 52 and number them 1 through 9 we have centered our intuitive energy.

Creature Teachers

1. Ant
2. Antelope
3. Armadillo
4. Badger
5. Bat
6. Bear
7. Beaver
8. Bee
9. Buffalo
10. Butterfly
11. Chicken
12. Cow
13. Coyote
14. Crow
15. Deer
16. Dog
17. Dolphin
18. Dragonfly
19. Eagle
20. Elk
21. Fox
22. Frog
23. Goat
24. Grouse
25. Hawk
26. Heron
27. Horse
28. Hummingbird
29. Lizard
30. Lynx
31. Moose
32. Mountain Lion
33. Mouse
34. Opossum
35. Otter
36. Owl
37. Porcupine
38. Rabbit
39. Raccoon
40. Raven
41. Sheep
42. Skunk
43. Snake
44. Snipe
45. Spider
46. Squirrel
47. Swan
48. Turkey
49. Turtle
50. Weasel
51. Whale
52. Wolf

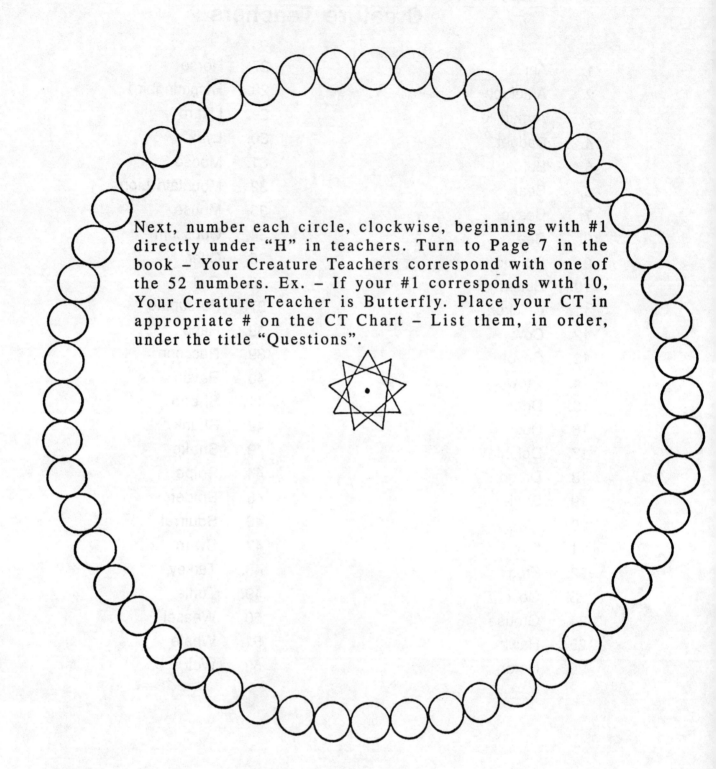

Next, number each circle, clockwise, beginning with #1 directly under "H" in teachers. Turn to Page 7 in the book – Your Creature Teachers correspond with one of the 52 numbers. Ex. – If your #1 corresponds with 10, Your Creature Teacher is Butterfly. Place your CT in appropriate # on the CT Chart – List them, in order, under the title "Questions".

Randomly select 9 circles and number them 1 thru 9.

How to Use This Circle

1]   Have Seeker of Truth randomly number nine circles 1-9.

2]   Starting with the circle directly below the "H" in the word "Teachers," number the circles 1-52 clockwise around the outside.

3]   Using the Creature Teachers chart, select the Creature Teacher which corresponds to the number selected. e.g.- If the seeker placed #1 in circle #10 then the first Creature Teacher is Butterfly.

4]   After the nine Creature Teachers have been found, place each one on the Creature Teachers wheel chart in order as follows:

> #1 in the East   #6 in the Below
> #2 in the South   #7 in the Within
> #3 in the West   #8 in Love
> #4 in the North   #9 in Peace
> #5 in the Above

5]   Locate the questions below the wheel and list the Creature Teachers according to the number as follows:

> 1)   Why?   - (CT #1)
> 2)   How?   - (CT #2)
> 3)   Who?   - (CT #3)
> 4)   Where?   - (CT #4)
> 5)   When?   - (CT #5)
> 6)   What?   - (CT #6)
> 7)   While   - (CT #7)
> 8)   This   - (CT #8)
> 9)   That   - (CT #9)

6]   Set aside this chart for later use.

7]   Locate the Creature Teachers spreadsheet on pages 24-25.

8]   Write in the Creature Teachers on the provided lines across the top 1-9.

9] Down the left side of the spreadsheet are listed the monitors according to the Cycle of Truth:

Learn	Love
Honor	Serve
Know	Live
See	Work
Hear	Share
Speak	Thank

10] After the monitors are listed the Creature Teachers' Contribution and gifts of the four directions:

North-	Wisdom
East-	Inspiration
South-	Lessons
West-	Future

11] Fill in the spreadsheet with the personal gifts revealed by each Creature Teacher by following the next few steps.

12] Locate the qualities of each Creature Teacher. (CT's are listed in alphabetical order.)

13] Each page includes:

a)   the contribution

b)   the description of monitor and place on the Wisdom Wheel of Truth.

14] Below the Wheel of Truth is the Wisdom Core which contains the gifts of the four directions for that Creature Teacher.

15] Fill in the spreadsheet using the monitors located on the Wisdom Wheel, the contribution, and directional gifts from the Wisdom Core for the Creature Teacher. Repeat for each Creature Teacher 1-9.

16] Locate the page entitled "Questions for Creature Teachers."

17] Questions are listed in 12 categories, A-L.

18] Place words from the spreadsheet next to the appropriate question. e.g.- word A-1 on the spreadsheet goes with question A1. (Words on the spreadsheet are labeled below the line.) Place all labeled words on the sheet.

19] Locate the page entitled "Personal Cycles of Truth based on Creature Teachers."

20] Intuitively select a word from category A on the "Questions" sheet. Mark it with a check mark.

21] Place the chosen word into the first blank on the left side of the Cycles of Truth sheet. Repeat steps 20-21 for each category, A-L.

22] When 12 words have been selected (one from each category), then write the across the top of the sheet in the form of a sentence. Add no connecting words, but punctuate to give the sentence its wisdom.

23] Using the lines at the bottom of the sheet, begin listing the words in the following way:

    1 Subject: (Word #1) (Word #4) (Word #7) (Word #10)
    3 Result: (Word #2) (Word #5) (Word #8) (Word #11)
    2 Process: (Word #3) (Word #6) (Word #9) (Word #12)

24] Read each category of words in the following way:

    The subject is: (1 Subject)
    The process is: (2 Process)
    The result is: (3 Result)

25] Place each word on to the Cycle of Truth Wheel beginning with word #1 from the entire list of 12 and placing it at "1 o'clock" on the wheel. Continue with word #2 at "2 o'clock" and so on.

26] Place the monitors of the Cycle of Truth in their proper places around the inside of the wheel. (Learn, Honor, Know, etc.)

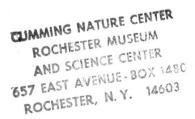

27] Repeat this process from step 20 using the Personal Pathway of Peace sheet. The words will be chosen from the three remaining words in each category A-L on the spreadsheet. When filling in the wheel for the Pathway of Peace, begin at the South (6 o'clock) which corresponds to Faith with word #1.

28] Repeat from step 20 using the Why Am I Here? sheet. This follows the same pattern as the Cycles of Truth. The words are chosen from the remaining two words in categories A-L

29] Repeat once more from step 20 using the What is My Future? sheet. This follows the same process as the Pathway of Peace. The single remaining word in each category A-L is used to fill in the sheet.

30] Return to the Creature Teachers wheel sheet and fill in the contribution of each Creature Teacher 1-9. Write them in the form of a sentence as in step 22. Divide them into categories as in step 23 and read their wisdom.

31] Return to the spreadsheet and have the Seeker search for duplicate words.

Triplicate or more-   Strong personal characteristics

Duplicate-   attracting these qualities as
                       teaching tools for self-expression

32] Using the Duplicates, create a sentence as in step 22 and then categorize the words as in step 23 and read their wisdom.

33] We suggest great value in finding as many definitions as possible for meanings of the words indicated in the contributions.

Interpretation of Creature Teachers Chart			Interpretation of Earthpath	
5	Above	= T	3	West
4	North	= R	8	Love
7	Within	= U	7	Within
2	South	= T	9	Peace
6	Below	= H	1	Inspiration

Questions corresponding to animals
Creature Teacher Contribution

1	Why	1	Subject
2	How	2	Result
3	Who	3	Process
4	Where		
5	When		
6	What		
7	While		
8	This		
9	That		

We thank our Ancestors and All our relations.

Yehwehnode
She Whose Voice Rides on the Winds

Note: 33 means double change
      6 means sharing through speaking the truth
Da Naho

On the following pages is an example completed up through the Personal Cycles of Truth. We trust that this will help to clear up any questions concerning the method of using this manual.

CREATURE TEACHERS

Example

Randomly select 9 circles and number them 1 thru 9

5. Above
Wisdom/Health   *Eagle*

Example

4. North
Gratitude   *Dolphin*

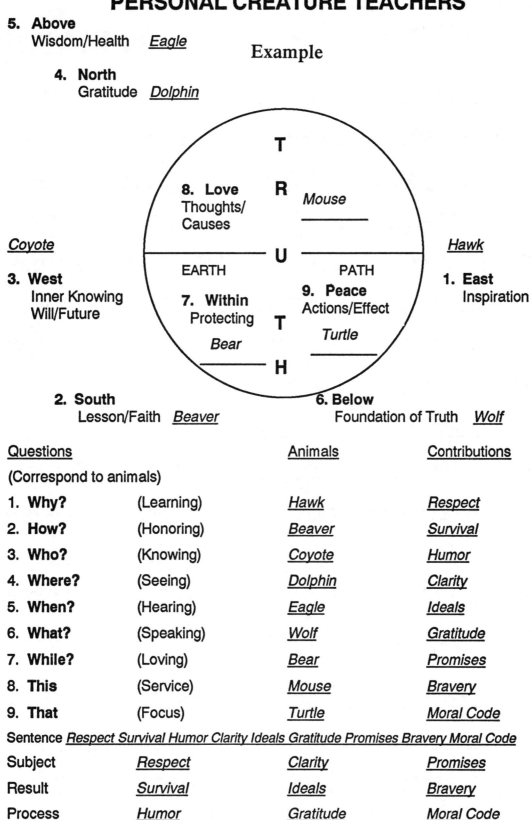

Coyote

3. West
Inner Knowing
Will/Future

Hawk

1. East
Inspiration

2. South
Lesson/Faith   *Beaver*

6. Below
Foundation of Truth   *Wolf*

Questions		Animals	Contributions
(Correspond to animals)			
1. **Why?**	(Learning)	*Hawk*	*Respect*
2. **How?**	(Honoring)	*Beaver*	*Survival*
3. **Who?**	(Knowing)	*Coyote*	*Humor*
4. **Where?**	(Seeing)	*Dolphin*	*Clarity*
5. **When?**	(Hearing)	*Eagle*	*Ideals*
6. **What?**	(Speaking)	*Wolf*	*Gratitude*
7. **While?**	(Loving)	*Bear*	*Promises*
8. **This**	(Service)	*Mouse*	*Bravery*
9. **That**	(Focus)	*Turtle*	*Moral Code*

Sentence *Respect Survival Humor Clarity Ideals Gratitude Promises Bravery Moral Code*

Subject	*Respect*	*Clarity*	*Promises*
Result	*Survival*	*Ideals*	*Bravery*
Process	*Humor*	*Gratitude*	*Moral Code*

Copyright © 1994 Twylah Nitsch

SENTENCE: Example

CREATURE

	Hawk 1	Beaver 2	Coyote 3	Dolphin 4
CONTRIBUTIONS:	Respect	Survival	Humor	Clarity
1. LEARN	Change F-1	Reason	Assimilating	Advancement
2. HONOR	Decisions	Gifts J-1	Choice	Cleansing
3. KNOW	Intuition	Clarity	Understanding F-2	Concession
4. SEE	Messenger E-1	Lessons	Trust	Composure H-1
5. HEAR	Observations	Adaptation E-2	Bonding	Meditation
6. SPEAK	Reality	Justice	Joy K-2	Repitition L-1
7. LOVE	Recognition	Endurance	Thoughtfulness G-3	Representing H-2
8. SERVE	Review	Versatility H-3	Seeking	Resounding
9. LIVE	Responsibilties H-4	Friendship	Service	Renewing K-1
10. WORK	Situation	Alignment	Skills G-4	Reporting
11. SHARE	Symbols	Enjoyment J-2	Teaching	Responding
12. THANK	Truth L-2	Harmony	Watching	Reviving
WISDOM	Partnership	Regard	Obedience	Restitution
INSPIRATION	Confirmation	Equality	Kinship	Redeeming
LESSONS	Granted	Unity	Justice	Refining
FUTURE	Approval	Steadfast	Observation	Recovery

TEACHERS

Eagle 5	Wolf 6	Bear 7	Mouse 8	Turtle 9
Ideals	Gratitude	Promises	Bravery	Moral Code
Balance B-1	Stillness	Advisement	Cautious	Survival I-1
Comfort B-2	Unity	Concern	Adaptability I-2	Living
Discipline B-3	Organization	Credibility G-1	Compatibility	Experience
Sincerity B-4	Orientation G-2	Independence	Effectability K-3	Reflection L-4
Purity A-1	Sensitivity	Depandability	Instinctively	Serenity
Inspiration A-2	Song I-3	Love J-3	Courageous	Worthiness
Integration A-3	Family L-3	Effort J-4	Sociability	Reputation
Revelation A-4	Foresight	Adoption	Agreement E-3	Integrity
Restoration C-1	Intuition I-4	Restoration	Curiosity	Efficiency E-4
Spirit C-2	Prophecy	Balance F-3	Scrutiny	Persistence
Ritual C-3	Benevolence	Colleagues	Regularity K-4	Peace
Support C-4	Therapy	Healing	Upright	Continutiy F-4
Grouping D-1	Structure	Sanction	Genuine	Growth
Character D-2	Truth	Acquistion	Inventive	Consolation
Definition D-3	Magnetism	Security	Confirmation	Renewal
Knowledge D-4	Philosophy	Fellowship	Security	Approval

QUESTIONS

FOR CREATURE TEACHERS

Example

Identification: List A

A1	Who am I?	*Purity*
A2	From where did I come?	*Inspiration*
A3	Why am I here?	*Integration*
A4	What is my future?	*Revelation*

Procedure: List B

B1	Am I happy in what I am doing?	*Balance*
B2	What am I doing to add to Peace and contentment?	*Comfort*
B3	What am I doing to add to the confusion?	*Discipline*
B4	How will I be remembered when I am gone?	*Sincerity*

What is my Contribution? List C

C1	Why do I honor the Truth?	*Restoration*
C2	How do I hear the Truth?	*Spirit*
C3	Where do I serve the Truth?	*Ritual*
C4	When do I share the Truth?	*Support*

What is my Achievement in Life? List D

D1	What is my life goal?	*Grouping*
D2	What is my unity?	*Character*
D3	What is my equality?	*Definition*
D4	What is my eternity?	*Knowledge*

How do I Reinforce my Gifts? List E

E1	Through my inner knowing of Truth (Challenge)	*Messenger*
E2	Through my intuitive speaking of Truth (Change)	*Adaptation*
E3	Through my eternal love of Truth (Choice)	*Agreement*
E4	Through my creative work in Love (Commitment)	*Efficiency*

Self-Awareness: List F

F1	Spiritual Truth	(Learning)	*Change*
F2	Mental Truth	(Knowing)	*Understanding*
F3	Physical Truth	(Working)	*Balance*
F4	Emotional Truth	(Thanking)	*Continuity*

Role Model: List G

G1	Need the Truth	(Know)	*Credibility*
G2	Image the Truth	(See)	*Orientation*
G3	Expression of Truth	(Love)	*Thoughtfulness*
G4	Cooperation in Truth	(Work)	*Skills*

Social Status/Skill: List H

H1	Nurturing the Truth	(See)	*Composure*
H2	Complementing the Truth	(Love)	*Representing*
H3	Representing the Truth	(Serve)	*Versatility*
H4	Affirming the Truth	(Live)	*Responsibilities*

What Characteristics are Most Pronounced for Developing Self-Esteem: List I

I1	Addressing the Truth	(Learn)	*Survival*
I2	Perform the Truth	(Honor)	*Adaptability*
I3	Perceiving the Truth	(Speak)	*Song*
I4	Comprehending the Truth	(Live)	*Intuition*

Where is my Comfort? List J

J1	How do I honor my comfort?	(Honor)	*Gifts*
J2	When do I share my comfort?	(Share)	*Enjoyment*
J3	Why do I speak my comfort?	(Speak)	*Love*
J4	What is my comfort?	(Love)	*Effort*

What is my Knowledge? List K

K1	Why do I need Knowledge?	(Live)	*Renewing*
K2	How do I communicate my Knowledge?	(Speak)	*Joy*
K3	When do I accept my Knowledge?	(Hear)	*Instinctively*
K4	Where do I gain my Knowledge?	(Share)	*Regularity*

What is my Gratitude? List L

L1	Where do I express my Gratitude?	(Speak)	*Repetition*
L2	When do I feel Gratitude?	(Thank)	*Truth*
L3	How do I show my Gratitude?	(Love)	*Family*
L4	Why do I live in Gratitude?	(See)	*Reflection*

Sentence: *Revelation Sincerity Ritual, Knowledge Messenger Balance, Credibility Versatility Survival, Love Instinctively Truth*

PERSONAL WISDOM WHEEL
Based on CYCLES OF TRUTH
Example

Learn my Identity	*Revelation*	A4
Honor my Procedure	*Sincerity*	B4
Know my Contribution	*Ritual*	C3
See my Achievement	*Knowledge*	D4
Hear my Reinforcement	*Messenger*	E1
Speak my Self-Awareness	*Balance*	F3
Love my Role Model	*Credibility*	G1
Serve my Social Status/Skill	*Versatility*	H3
Live my Personal Characteristic	*Survival*	I1
Work my Comfort	*Love*	J3
Share my Knowledge	*Instinctively*	K3
Thank my Gratitude	*Truth*	L2

Subject 1:	*Revelation*	*Knowledge*	*Credibility*	*Love*
Result 3:	*Sincerity*	*Messenger*	*Versatility*	*Instinctively*
Process 2:	*Ritual*	*Balance*	*Survival*	*Truth*

PERSONAL
CYCLES of TRUTH
Example

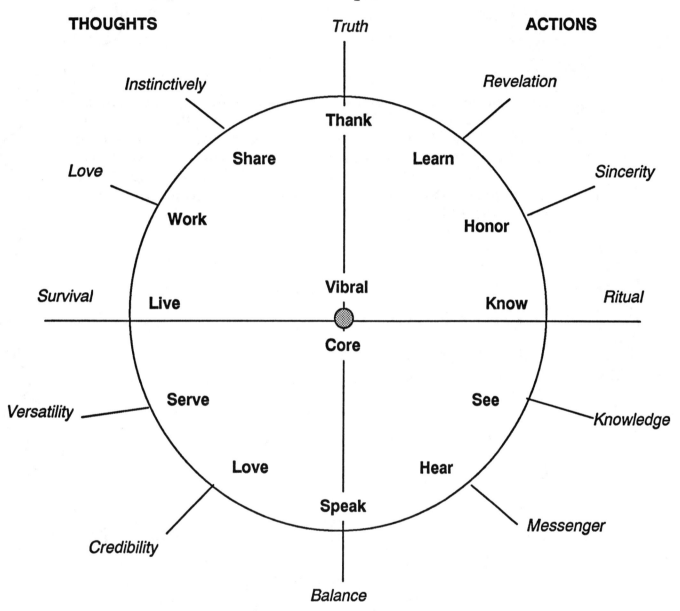

THOUGHTS   *Truth*   **ACTIONS**

Instinctively

Thank

Revelation

Share   **Learn**

Love

Work   *Sincerity*

Honor

Vibral

Survival   **Live**   **Know**   *Ritual*

Core

Serve   **See**

Versatility   *Knowledge*

Love   **Hear**

Credibility   **Speak**   *Messenger*

Balance

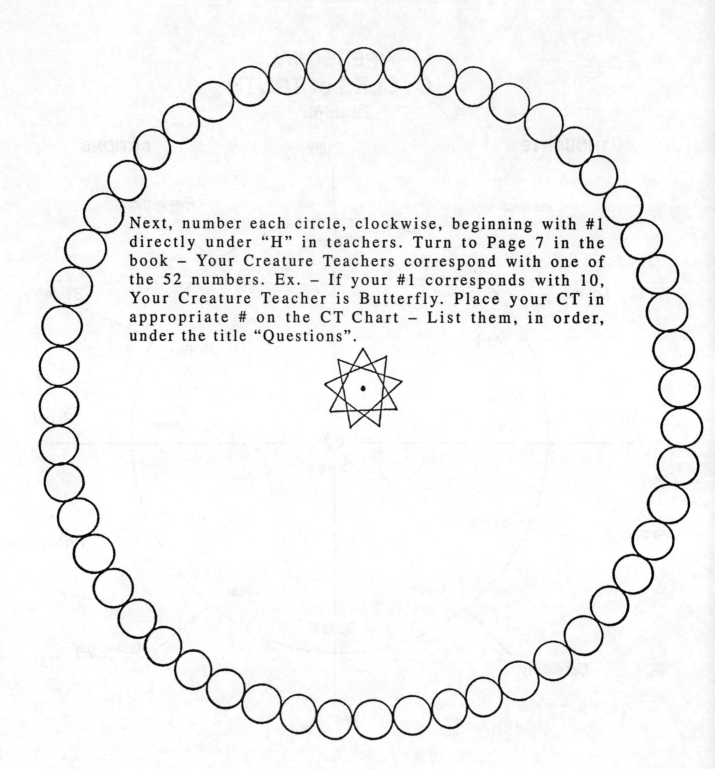

Next, number each circle, clockwise, beginning with #1 directly under "H" in teachers. Turn to Page 7 in the book – Your Creature Teachers correspond with one of the 52 numbers. Ex. – If your #1 corresponds with 10, Your Creature Teacher is Butterfly. Place your CT in appropriate # on the CT Chart – List them, in order, under the title "Questions".

Randomly select 9 circles and number them 1 thru 9.

5. Above
Wisdom/Health _____

4. North
Gratitude _____

T

R

8. Love
Thoughts/
Causes _____

_____ U _____   _____

EARTH   PATH

3. West   **1. East**
Inner Knowing   **9. Peace**   Inspiration
Will/Future   **7. Within**   Actions/Effect
Protecting   _____

T
_____

H

2. South   **6. Below**
Lesson/Faith _____   Foundation of Truth _____

Questions		Animals	Contributions
(Correspond to animals)			
1. **Why?**	(Learning)	_____	_____
2. **How?**	(Honoring)	_____	_____
3. **Who?**	(Knowing)	_____	_____
4. **Where?**	(Seeing)	_____	_____
5. **When?**	(Hearing)	_____	_____
6. **What?**	(Speaking)	_____	_____
7. **While?**	(Loving)	_____	_____
8. **This**	(Service)	_____	_____
9. **That**	(Focus)	_____	_____
Sentence _____			
Subject		_____	_____
Result		_____	_____
Process		_____	_____

SENTENCE:

CREATURE

	1	2	3	4
CONTRIBUTIONS:				
1. LEARN	F-1			
2. HONOR		J-1		
3. KNOW			F-2	
4. SEE	E-1			H-1
5. HEAR		E-2		
6. SPEAK			K-2	L-1
7. LOVE			G-3	H-2
8. SERVE		H-3		
9. LIVE	H-4			K-1
10. WORK			G-4	
11. SHARE		J-2		
12. THANK	L-2			
WISDOM				
INSPIRATION				
LESSONS				
FUTURE				

TEACHERS

5	6	7	8	9
B-1				I-1
B-2			I-2	
B-3		G-1		
B-4	G-2			L-4
A-1			K-3	
A-2	I-3	J-3		
A-3	L-3	J-4		
A-4			E-3	
C-1	I-4			E-4
C-2		F-3		
C-3			K-4	
C-4				F-4
D-1				
D-2				
D-3				
D-4				

QUESTIONS

FOR CREATURE TEACHERS

Identification: List A

A1	Who am I?	_____
A2	From where did I come?	_____
A3	Why am I here?	_____
A4	What is my future?	_____

Procedure: List B

B1	Am I happy in what I am doing?	_____
B2	What am I doing to add to Peace and contentment?	_____
B3	What am I doing to add to the confusion?	_____
B4	How will I be remembered when I am gone?	_____

What is my Contribution? List C

C1	Why do I honor the Truth?	_____
C2	How do I hear the Truth?	_____
C3	Where do I serve the Truth?	_____
C4	When do I share the Truth?	_____

What is my Achievement in Life? List D

D1	What is my life goal?	_____
D2	What is my unity?	_____
D3	What is my equality?	_____
D4	What is my eternity?	_____

How do I Reinforce my Gifts? List E

E1	Through my inner knowing of Truth (Challenge)	_____
E2	Through my intuitive speaking of Truth (Change)	_____
E3	Through my eternal love of Truth (Choice)	_____
E4	Through my creative work in Love (Commitment)	_____

Self-Awareness: List F

F1	Spiritual Truth	(Learning)	_____
F2	Mental Truth	(Knowing)	_____
F3	Physical Truth	(Working)	_____
F4	Emotional Truth	(Thanking)	_____

Role Model: List G

G1	Need the Truth	(Know)	_____
G2	Image the Truth	(See)	_____
G3	Expression of Truth	(Love)	_____
G4	Cooperation in Truth	(Work)	_____

Social Status/Skill: List H

H1	Nurturing the Truth	(See)	_____
H2	Complementing the Truth	(Love)	_____
H3	Representing the Truth	(Serve)	_____
H4	Affirming the Truth	(Live)	_____

What Characteristics are Most Pronounced for Developing Self-Esteem: List I

I1	Addressing the Truth	(Learn)	_____
I2	Perform the Truth	(Honor)	_____
I3	Perceiving the Truth	(Speak)	_____
I4	Comprehending the Truth	(Live)	_____

Where is my Comfort? List J

J1	How do I honor my comfort?	(Honor)	_____
J2	When do I share my comfort?	(Share)	_____
J3	Why do I speak my comfort?	(Speak)	_____
J4	What is my comfort?	(Love)	_____

What is my Knowledge? List K

K1	Why do I need Knowledge?	(Live)	_____
K2	How do I communicate my Knowledge?	(Speak)	_____
K3	When do I accept my Knowledge?	(Hear)	_____
K4	Where do I gain my Knowledge?	(Share)	_____

What is my Gratitude? List L

L1	Where do I express my Gratitude?	(Speak)	_____
L2	When do I feel Gratitude?	(Thank)	_____
L3	How do I show my Gratitude?	(Love)	_____
L4	Why do I live in Gratitude?	(See)	_____

Sentence:

PERSONAL WISDOM WHEEL
Based on CYCLES OF TRUTH

Learn my Identity _____

Honor my Procedure _____

Know my Contribution _____

See my Achievement _____

Hear my Reinforcement _____

Speak my Self-Awareness _____

Love my Role Model _____

Serve my Social Status/Skill _____

Live my Personal Characteristic _____

Work my Comfort _____

Share my Knowledge _____

Thank my Gratitude _____

Subject 1: _____ _____ _____ _____

Result   3: _____ _____ _____ _____

Process 2: _____ _____ _____ _____

PERSONAL
CYCLES of TRUTH

THOUGHTS

ACTIONS

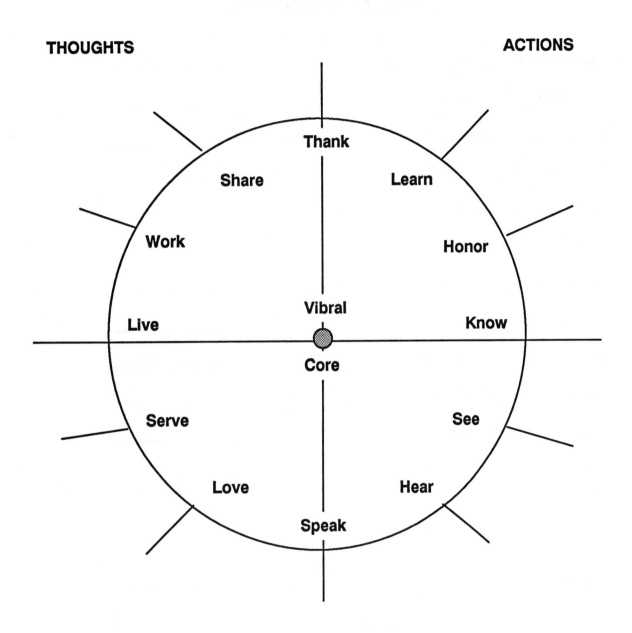

Thank

Share

Learn

Work

Honor

Vibral

Live

Know

Core

Serve

See

Love

Hear

Speak

Sentence:

PERSONAL PATHWAY OF PEACE
Based on PATHWAY OF PEACE

Faith through Self-Awareness   _____

Love through Role Model   _____

Intuition through Social Status/Skill   _____

Will through Personal Characteristic   _____

Creativity through Comfort   _____

Magnetism through Knowledge   _____

Wisdom through Gratitude   _____

Learning through Identity   _____

Honoring through Procedure   _____

Knowing through Contribution   _____

Seeing through Achievement   _____

Hearing through Reinforcement   _____

Subject   1:   _____   _____   _____   _____

Result   3:   _____   _____   _____   _____

Process   2:   _____   _____   _____   _____

Pathway of Peace

THOUGHTS

ACTIONS

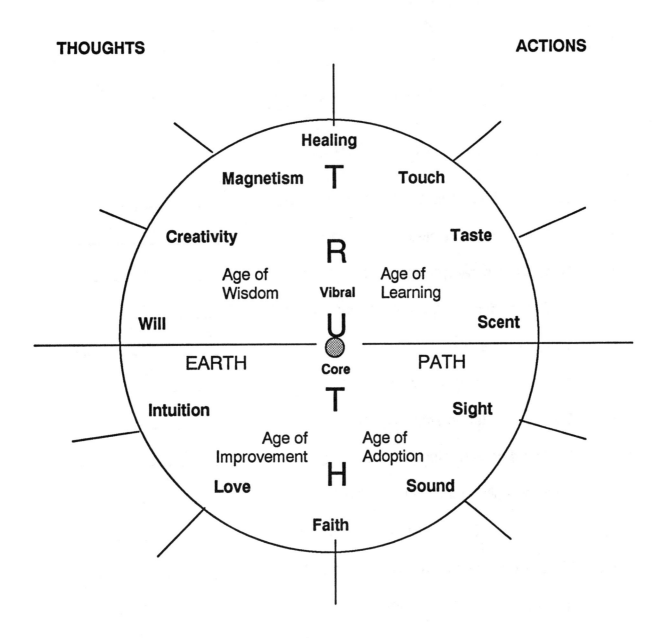

Healing

Magnetism

Touch

T

Creativity

Taste

R

Age of Wisdom

Vibral

Age of Learning

Will

U

Scent

Core

EARTH

PATH

T

Intuition

Sight

Age of Improvement

Age of Adoption

H

Love

Sound

Faith

Sentence:

WHY AM I HERE?

1. To Learn about promise/expectation through _____

2. To Honor intention/integrity through _____

3. To Know accuracy/organization through _____

4. To See confirmation/transformation through _____

5. To Hear timing/thinking through _____

6. To Speak of image/model through _____

7. To Love challenge/efficiency through _____

8. To Serve growth/reform through _____

9. To Live challenge/efficiency through _____

10. To Work with opportunity/ambition through _____

11. To Share direction/development through _____

12. To Thank flexibility/agreement through _____

Subject 1: _____ _____ _____ _____

Result   3: _____ _____ _____ _____

Process 2: _____ _____ _____ _____

WHY AM I HERE?
Based on
Cycles of Truth

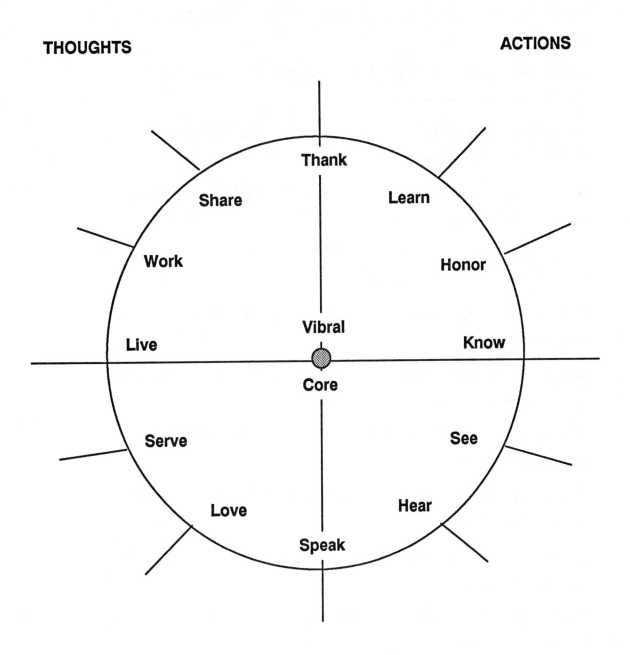

THOUGHTS

ACTIONS

Thank

Share

Learn

Work

Honor

Vibral

Live

Know

Core

Serve

See

Love

Hear

Speak

Sentence:

WHAT IS MY FUTURE?

Faith in the future through persuasion/emotion expressing
_____

Love the future through being supportive/compatible expressing _____

Intuition in the future through being discerning/intelligent expressing _____

Will in the future through choosing/reliability expressing _____

Creativity for the future through activity/foresight expressing _____

Magnetism in the future through sharing/strategy expressing _____

Wisdom in the future through healing/wholeness expressing _____

Touch the future through inspiration/goals expressing _____

Taste the future through deliberation/selection expressing _____

Scent the future through accuracy/commitment expressing _____

Sight the future through impressing/self-esteem expressing _____

Sound the future through harmony/coordination expressing _____

Subject 1: _____ _____ _____ _____
Result 3: _____ _____ _____ _____
Process 2: _____ _____ _____ _____

THOUGHTS

ACTIONS

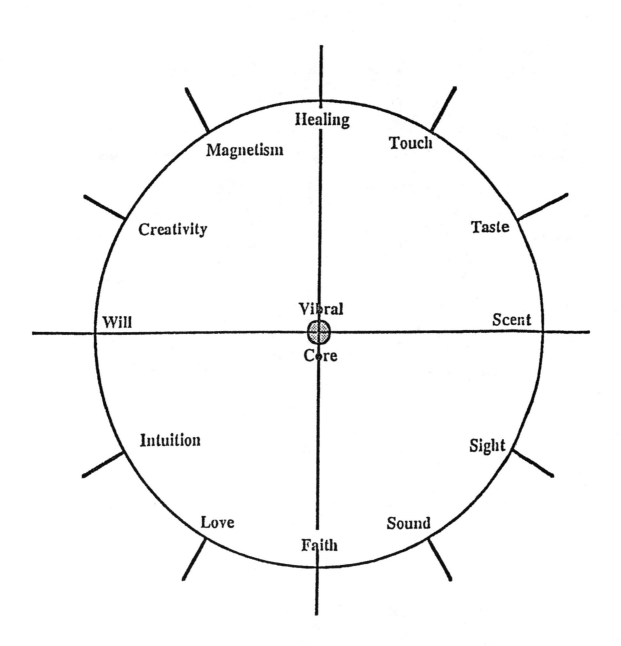

Ant

Contribution - Communication

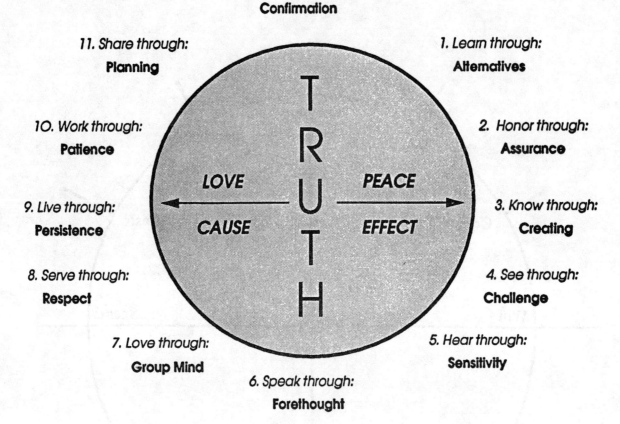

12. Thank through:
Confirmation

11. Share through:
Planning

1. Learn through:
Alternatives

10. Work through:
Patience

2. Honor through:
Assurance

LOVE | PEACE

TRUTH

CAUSE | EFFECT

9. Live through:
Persistence

3. Know through:
Creating

8. Serve through:
Respect

4. See through:
Challenge

7. Love through:
Group Mind

5. Hear through:
Sensitivity

6. Speak through:
Forethought

Core:

North
Wisdom through:
Transmitting

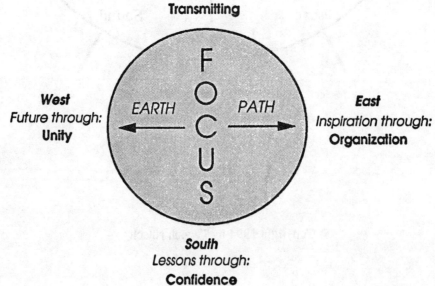

West
Future through:
Unity

EARTH | PATH

FOCUS

East
Inspiration through:
Organization

South
Lessons through:
Confidence

Ant

Decree of Communication

Communicating Truth is always tuned in,
It unites with inner peace that comes from within.

Many days and nights had visited Earthland before the Ant People came. When they emerged from Motherearth to find a new place to live, they ran in every direction blinded by the light of the Outer World. Fear entered their hearts as they scattered and strayed. Life had been different when they lived beneath the Earth where passageways safely guided their walk.

"Where is everybody?" they cried in desperation. No Ant Person answered their plea. The Ant People had lost their confidence after they entered the Outer World.

It happened that two straying Ants bumped into each other and they recognized by their feelers who they were. Instantly, confidence swelled their bodies. "Together we can feel our way and search for our relatives," they decided. One followed the other as they guided their walk -- taking turns while leading. Soon, other Ants fell into line and confidence filled their hearts. It wasn't long before their feelers connected them with other Ant bodies. This touching created a valuable system of communication.

After all the strayed Ants had been united, they held a Council. The Ants decided they had to focus on seeing to adjust to their blindness in the Outer Earth environment. Time passed while every Ant Person adjusted their seeing. During this time, Motherearth cared for their needs.

"It's time for another Ant Council," whispered Motherearth. Every Ant heard the whisper that came from their caretaker. The Ant Council convened to listen to Earth's Decree:

The Light of Truth is based upon option,
It's time to decide on adoption.
Begin the foundation from inner worth,
And build the passageways to Outer Earth.

Motherearth has spoken!

After this message was received, the Ant People became Earthmovers and built huge mounds as Ant Colonies. These Earth Mounds provided the right sized passageways from Inner Earth to the Outer Earth.

As time passed, the Ant People established an organized system of communication that has become a stable way of life.

Da Naho!

Antelope

Contribution - Listening

12. Thank through:
Touching

11. Share through:
Integrity

1. Learn through:
Reason

10. Work through:
Interest

2. Honor through:
Comforting

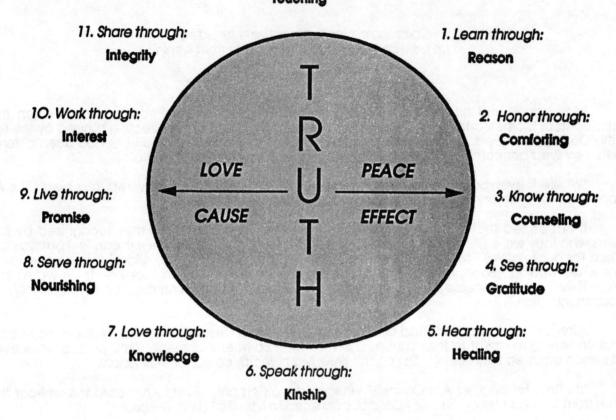

LOVE   *PEACE*

T R U T H

CAUSE   *EFFECT*

9. Live through:
Promise

3. Know through:
Counseling

8. Serve through:
Nourishing

4. See through:
Gratitude

7. Love through:
Knowledge

5. Hear through:
Healing

6. Speak through:
Kinship

Core:

North
Wisdom through:
Giving

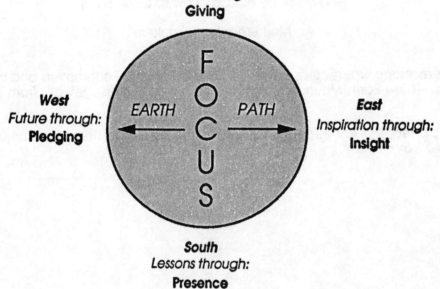

F O C U S

EARTH   *PATH*

West
Future through:
Pledging

East
Inspiration through:
Insight

South
Lessons through:
Presence

Antelope
Decree of Listening

Listen, listen is the gift of thought,
It must be earned, it cannot be bought.
Listening is a latent talent,
Practice listening makes it present.

Many Moons ago, a Council convened where hoofed and cud chewing Animal People attended. Antelope came to meet their relatives -- Goat, Sheep and Cow. However, as they talked with each other, their chewing prevented them from listening. The louder they talked the less they could listen. When the Thunder People heard all the noise, they came to investigate. They noticed these hoofed and chewing Animal People spent most of their time eating and chewing.

"Are these chewing Animal People planning to out noise us?" the Thunderers asked.
"This cannot be," they agreed.

Hinoh, the Thunder Chief, made the following announcement:

Rumble, rumble from the distant past,
Listen for reason has come at last.
Eating and chewing seals the Vibral Core,
No one listens to the Truth anymore.

The Antelope shook their heads to open their ears for they possessed clear thinking. This problem was fast becoming serious because the Antelope preferred to chew rather than listen. As time passed, this problem worsened and the Antelopes were losing their gift of reason.

The Antelope Elders said "We must awaken our listening". It was decided to send four Youngers of their People into the Four Directions to awaken their listening.

The first Younger went North to dream Antelope Wisdom. The second Younger went to the East to Listen within. The third Younger went to the South to Hear what the other Antelopes were saying. The fourth Younger to hear about Antelope's future. When each Antelope reached the assigned destination, they all became tired and laid down to rest.

Sleep overtook them and Dreams gave them direction. When they awoke from their sleep, they felt a strange sensation at the crown of their heads. It frightened them. At the moment they wanted to flee, a gentle voice whispered into their ears.

The one at the North heard, "I am your Dream of Wisdom, your inner vision."
The one at the East heard, "I am your Inspiration, your listening revelation."
The one at the South heard, "I am your new Image, your faithful sage."
The one at the West heard, "I am your Reason -- your inner freedom."
Presently these voices within revealed:

Harmony is your gift of Hearing,
While it guides you through the peaceful door.
Reason is the Truth for Listening,
As Peace enters at the Vibral Core.

When the four Younger Antelopes returned, they surprised all their relatives for each one wore two horns - one for Listening and one for Reasoning. To this day, the Antelope reminds all Creature Beings of this gift to listen and reason. As a result, Antelope awakens the action that brings about reason. This action brings on comfort for learning how to listen within.

Da Nahol

Armadillo

Contribution - Grounding

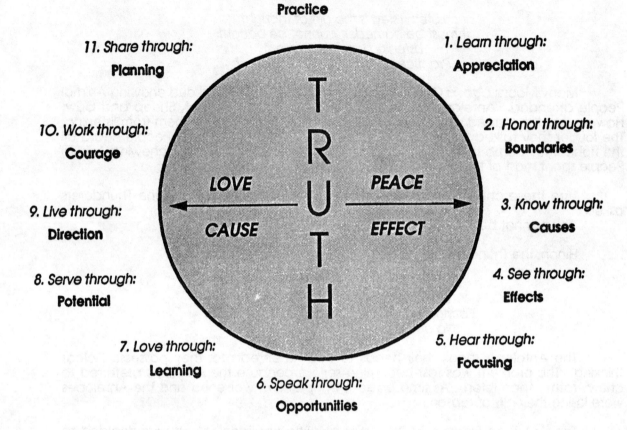

12. Thank through:
Practice

11. Share through:
Planning

1. Learn through:
Appreciation

10. Work through:
Courage

2. Honor through:
Boundaries

9. Live through:
Direction

3. Know through:
Causes

8. Serve through:
Potential

4. See through:
Effects

7. Love through:
Learning

5. Hear through:
Focusing

6. Speak through:
Opportunities

In circle: TRUTH — LOVE — PEACE — CAUSE — EFFECT

Core:

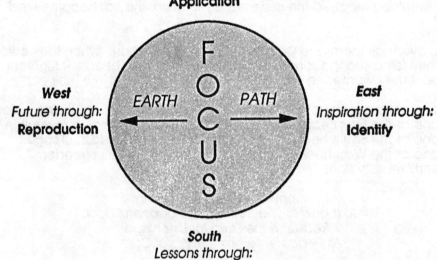

North
Wisdom through:
Application

West
Future through:
Reproduction

East
Inspiration through:
Identify

South
Lessons through:
Skills

In circle: FOCUS — EARTH — PATH

Armadillo
Decree of Grounding

It has been said by those who can foresee,
All Beings are safe within a decree.
It forms a Truth that sets them free,
To seek insight as a guarantee.

One day when Grandfather Sun shone on the nearby sea, Armadillo walked to water's edge to get a drink. Armadillo didn't notice that a huge wave was rolling toward the shore and when it crashed over the shoreline, it carried Armadillo toward the beach, between a cluster of rocks where his body became wedged.

"What are you doing here?" asked the Rock Person.

Armadillo, shocked at being held in fast, wiggled to and fro, only to be more firmly stuck between the rocks.

"Help me!" he gasped as the grip of the rocks choked him.

"Lie Still!" ordered the Rock Person. "False movements create boundaries that hinder your freedom. Be grateful your coat protects your inner being. You have a gift that keeps you grounded. Listen and learn!"

Armadillo stopped struggling and suddenly a giant wave poured over his body, lifting him into its frothy mouth and carried him out to sea. Armadillo rolled himself into a ball and when the wave rumbled to the shore, Armadillo rode the crest as it billowed inland, dropping him safely upon the sand. In the distance, he heard the Rock speak:

Roll and dance, oh mighty sea,
Surge and swell for Truth is free.
Appreciate boundaries one and all,
Ground all potentials by walking tall.

Armadillo realized that he had boundaries and, if necessary, he could roll with the Sea of Life. From that time, Armadillo's objective in growing was to appreciate the Truth of Wholeness by being grounded.

Armadillo slices in between,
Armadillo offers self-esteem,
It gives a sense of self
To keep from being shelved.
Armadillo brings upliftment,
By revealing one's boundary of commitment.

Da Naho!

Badger

Contribution - Centering

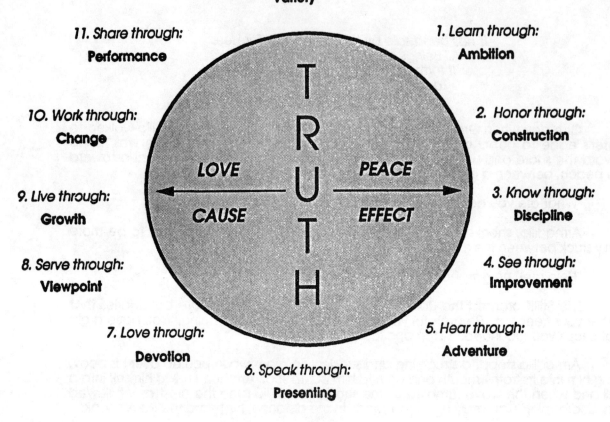

12. Thank through:
Variety

11. Share through:
Performance

1. Learn through:
Ambition

10. Work through:
Change

2. Honor through:
Construction

LOVE   *PEACE*

TRUTH

CAUSE   *EFFECT*

9. Live through:
Growth

3. Know through:
Discipline

8. Serve through:
Viewpoint

4. See through:
Improvement

7. Love through:
Devotion

5. Hear through:
Adventure

6. Speak through:
Presenting

Core:

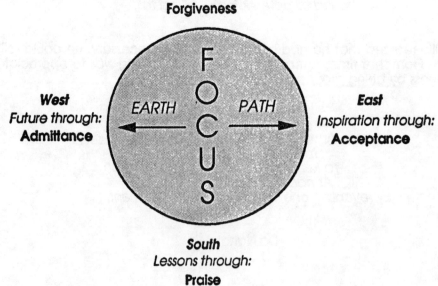

North
Wisdom through:
Forgiveness

West
Future through:
Admittance

EARTH   *PATH*

FOCUS

East
Inspiration through:
Acceptance

South
Lessons through:
Praise

Badger
Decree of Centering

What is the core of your Peace Wisdom?
What is your self-control?
What is your restoring lesson?
What is your major goal?

Many years ago when Motherearth was very young most Animals lived in Earth-dens for protection. In the beginning of human Earth Walk, our Ancestors also sought protection in the Earth. We emerged from the womb of Motherearth and when we end our Earth Walk, our bodies return to the Earth. Badger lives the same lifestyle.

Our Elders tell us that Badger is a most gifted Creature Being. His major gift is called "animal sensing," meaning sensitive to environmental influences and changes. Badger gives warning to all Creatures: when a severe storm is in the air, and when there are food shortages. Badger is dependable and all Earth's Creature Beings honor Badger for it's gifts of Sensitivity.

A time came when a strange feeling swept over Nature Land leaving the inhabitants in a state of lethargy. The feeling spread from one Creature to the next, causing their eyes to lose their sparkle. Badger was also affected by the peculiar illness.

Badger called a Council and asked other Badgers if they were suffering from the same sickness. While they counseled in wonderment, a strong wind came from the North and hovered over them. Presently a voice whistled through the trees:

Nature is the teacher for clarity of mind,
It's the healthiest gift that all Creatures can find.
There's no need for clogging the sources of living,
When clear thoughts restore the love of forgiving.

The Badgers were bewildered by this message. Suddenly, a foul smell filled the air and choked them. Their wisdom made them remain quiet.

The Clan Mother spoke to quiet their minds:

A decree we shall see before our eyes,
Seek the cause that is severing our ties.
The nose is the sensor directing the mind,
Locate the reason that reveals the sign.

The Badger possessed an analytical mind and soon discovered the Creatures had been drinking stagnant water from a nearby stream. Badger noticed that the stream, once clear and moving, was now choked with debris. A severe storm had clogged the flow and dying objects created a foul odor. The contamination was so gradual that the inhabitants who depended upon the water had not noticed its stench.

Badger had centered his thoughts upon the living conditions and learned that clean surroundings provide the principals for a healthy life style. Badger had received another gift of perception that changed his life and restored the health for all Creatures. Now life would be safer where there are Badgers.

Da Nahol

Bat

Contribution - Principles

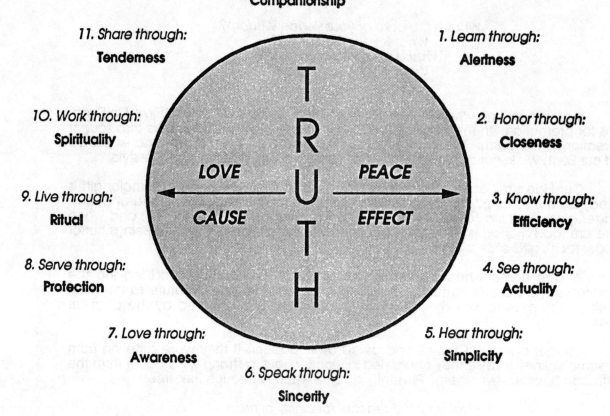

12. Thank through:
Companionship

11. Share through:
Tenderness

1. Learn through:
Alertness

10. Work through:
Spirituality

2. Honor through:
Closeness

9. Live through:
Ritual

3. Know through:
Efficiency

8. Serve through:
Protection

4. See through:
Actuality

7. Love through:
Awareness

5. Hear through:
Simplicity

6. Speak through:
Sincerity

LOVE — TRUTH — PEACE
CAUSE / EFFECT

Core:

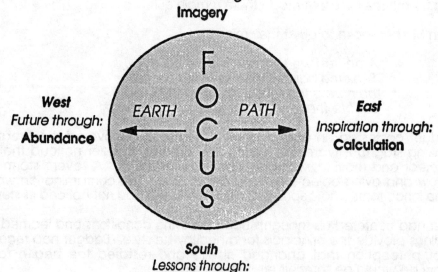

North
Wisdom through:
Imagery

West
Future through:
Abundance

East
Inspiration through:
Calculation

South
Lessons through:
Assimilation

FOCUS — EARTH / PATH

Bat

Decree of Principles

Let's state principles to keep a vow,
By providing gifts we can endow.
And nurturing friends as thoughts allow,
To foster love the best we know how.

Many Moons ago, the Creature Keepers held a Council at Sacred Mountain. Representatives from all Bird Clans and small animal Clans attended. The Creature Keepers protected the records of Clan honor so that the nature of each Clan could perpetuate their Sacred Place within the Earth's society.

Two Councils convened at the same time. One was the Council of Birds, the other, a Council of Small Animals. Suddenly, a rumble was heard coming from a distance. Lightning flashed and heavy rain descended from the Sky World. Sacred Mountain began to shake violently. The Bird People fled into the Sky World, while the Animal People scattered in every direction. Two Mouse representatives were thrown from where they stood and landed upon a vibrating rock.

When they surveyed their surroundings, they saw two wings hanging on the rock to which they clung. Quickly, they put the wings over their shoulders and soared into the surrounding space. Presently, a voice reached their ears from within their bodies, saying:

You have entered the space of choice,
Where living has a Sacred Voice.
Where flyers no longer fly,
And walkers no longer try.

Take heed and seek your need,
Reside within a creed.
Light turns into the night,
Right finds the inner sight.

Trust reveals the just,
Life unites with trust.

The air stilled, no sound could be heard. The flying Mice sought a flat protruding rock and clung to its sturdy surface. The Mice faced each other with questioning eyes.

One asked, "Did you hear a voice?"

"Yes," answered the second Mouse. "Let's make a vow to become whole right now," responded the other.

The Creature Keepers made their ritual of promise:

We fled by night -- led by inner sight,
Vowing to live through love.
Trust is our bond between love and peace,
That links below with above.

Death and rebirth, Bat Wisdom is used when one enters into Clarity Vision. The darkness becomes one's friend. Bat Wisdom introduces rituals and development of psychic gifts to confront one's own fears.

This is how the Mouse became the Bat. Their promise was the first ritual that united the Earth World with the Sky World and withinness makes them fearless. Their ritual is one of protection from above as well as from below.

Da Naho!

Bear

Contribution - Promises

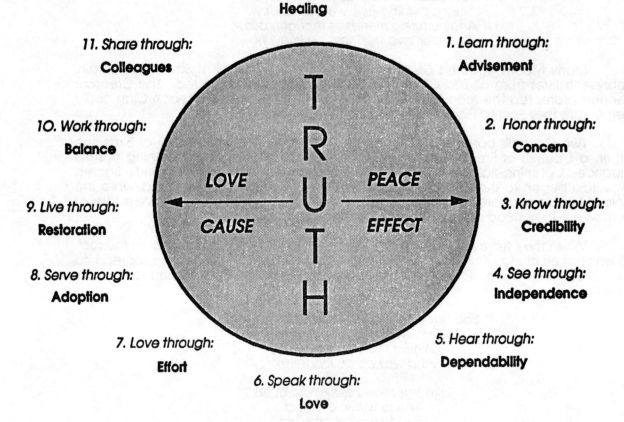

12. *Thank through:*
Healing

11. *Share through:*
Colleagues

1. *Learn through:*
Advisement

10. *Work through:*
Balance

2. *Honor through:*
Concern

LOVE — PEACE

9. *Live through:*
Restoration

CAUSE — EFFECT

3. *Know through:*
Credibility

8. *Serve through:*
Adoption

4. *See through:*
Independence

7. *Love through:*
Effort

5. *Hear through:*
Dependability

6. *Speak through:*
Love

Core:

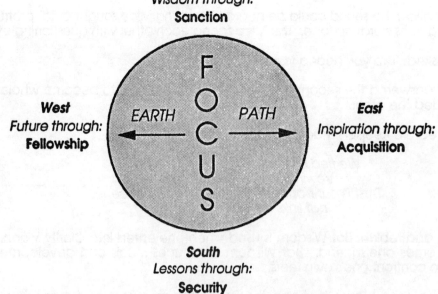

North
Wisdom through:
Sanction

West
Future through:
Fellowship

EARTH — PATH

East
Inspiration through:
Acquisition

South
Lessons through:
Security

Bear

Decree of Promises

Bear Wisdom reveals cause and effect,
By facing conditions with self-respect.
Promises spark loving from the heart,
Connecting with trust makes the best start.

In the center of the forest lived a Bear family with Twins; Dayeo, meaning he's busy, and Hakhowaneh, meaning he's a big eater. The Twins looked so much alike that the Forest Creatures couldn't tell them apart. Because of this, the Twins spent much of their time confusing the Creatures around them. They were lovable Twins and attracted all kinds of friends. However, a time came when the Twins were to enter the Outer Woods to learn about self-survival. The Twins knew that one of them would become the Bear Chief and the other would become the Spiritual Teacher.

The Bear Chief gave them some directions, saying, "You will enter the Outer Woods together and walk side by side until an experience separates you. Return after your first sleep in the Outer Woods

Dayeo and Hakhowaneh bounded off into the Outer Woods, unaware of what tests they would face. Soon they came to a fast flowing river. Without thinking of any consequences, they dashed into the turbulent water. The current picked them up so fast, they had no time to think. Suddenly, Dayeo became wedged between two giant rocks while Hakhowaneh slid toward a waterfall.

Slowly, Dayeo lifted himself from the rocks and groped his way to the shore while Hakhowaneh slid toward a rock slab saved from the rumbling waterfalls. A Hawk happened by and whispered into Hakhowaneh's ear saying "Follow me. I know where there is good food to strengthen your body." Hakhowaneh followed his friend who led him to a Honey Tree. "Welcome," said the Honey Tree. "Eat the honey the Bees are preparing. The food can restore your strength."

In the meantime, Dayeo laid upon the shore wondering what to do next. Soon, the same Hawk hovered over Dayeo and told him to find forest friends who would help him learn how to live with the Woodland Creatures.

Fall came and Dayeo had prepared for his long sleep. Hakhowaneh was having so much fun that he forgot to make his survival plans.

The Cold Chief arrived on schedule and covered the foolish Hakhowaneh with a white blanket. Spring came and it was time for Dayeo to meet his brother while Dayeo waited for Hakhowaneh who did not appear. A Hummingbird whispered to him that a sick Bear needed his help. Dayeo followed the Hummingbird and discovered that it was his Brother. With the help of all the Forest Friends, Hakhowaneh became strong again.

Dayeo and Hakhowaneh told of the experiences they had and how being truthful had warmed their bodies and the experiences that had created concern and pain. The Chief and their Mother were proud of their sons. Hakhowaneh told the Council that he was a foolish Bear who didn't honor his teachings. Therefore, his Brother should become Chief. Presently, a strong wind spoke:

The Bear who suffered the Winter's Cold,
Learned the lesson survival has told.
Dayeo becomes the Bear Chief and represents the Clan,
Hakhowaneh as Sachem will teach the Truth of the Land.

The Brothers restored their own gifts and were honored for sharing the lessons of the Outer Worlds.

Da Naho!

Beaver

Contribution - Survival

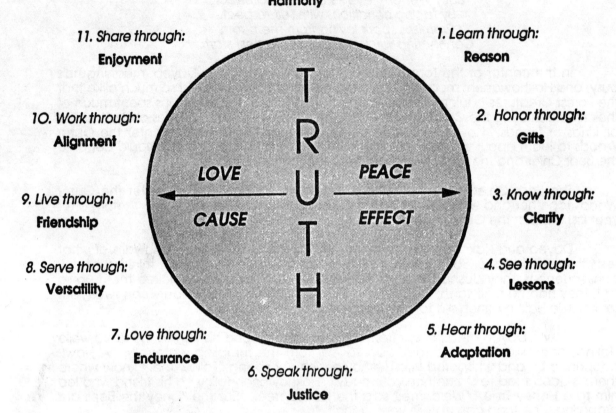

12. Thank through:
Harmony

11. Share through:
Enjoyment

1. Learn through:
Reason

10. Work through:
Alignment

2. Honor through:
Gifts

9. Live through:
Friendship

3. Know through:
Clarity

8. Serve through:
Versatility

4. See through:
Lessons

7. Love through:
Endurance

5. Hear through:
Adaptation

6. Speak through:
Justice

(Inside large circle: TRUTH / LOVE / PEACE / CAUSE / EFFECT)

Core:

North
Wisdom through:
Regard

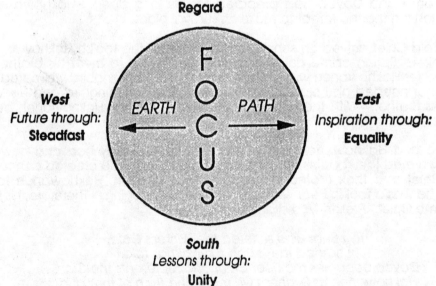

West
Future through:
Steadfast

East
Inspiration through:
Equality

(Inside circle: FOCUS / EARTH / PATH)

South
Lessons through:
Unity

Beaver
Decree of Survival

The Beaver foresees that life could be free,
So many were born that births were a spree.
The food became scarce and starving a dread,
A way had been set to save life instead.

Survival of the Fittest

Rivers and streams that spilled into the crystal lake above the Thunder Falls were filled with furry Beaver People moving silently toward the starting place to enter the race. Great preparations had gone into honoring strong bodies, clear minds and pure spirits to enter the Beaver race. The atmosphere was silent, in sacred anticipation. In the Sky World, the clouds, heavy with rain, waited for Hinoh the Thunder Chief to signal for the race to begin. Creature Beings of every kind selected their places to watch the race of survival.

The purpose of this unusual race was to solve a grave problem that had visited the Beaver Clans. Their population had exploded into great numbers so that food and lodging places had become scarce. Beaver Elders forewarned their Clans of the growing lack of cooperation. The need to honor the Sacred Places of other Creature People had been ignored. Hardship was spreading into other Clans.

The time had come for the greatest challenge to determine courage and endurance as survival of the fittest. Their future depended on this test. Every Beaver, whether young or old, entered this race. Creatures Beings of every kind lined the shores to watch the race of life. The spectators knew they would gain wisdom from the plight the Beaver People had brought upon themselves.

Beaver of all ages waited at the mouth of a great river that tumbled over the rocks leading to the edge of Thunder Falls. When Hinoh, the Thunder Chief, gave the signal, his strong voice unleashed the hold of the Cloud World and rain dropped in torrents upon the heads of the Beavers. Waves of Beaver bodies, hearty and brave, raced among the current toward the edge of Thunder Falls. Their strength sustained them as they moved along the rocks that led to the hungry mouth of the whirlpool below. They knew that survival depended upon their pure spirit.

Hungrily, the swirling waters ate whoever fell into its mouth. Chewing and swirling, it coughed up whoever had survived. Those who endured were the strongest and were rewarded by entering into the river of Peace, pure in body, heart, mind and spirit.

Life of abundance adds pounds to his weight,
The race of survival reveals ones fate.
Call out the weak to protect the breed,
Refine the stock that strength shall reseed.

Da Naho!

Bee

Contribution - Perserverance

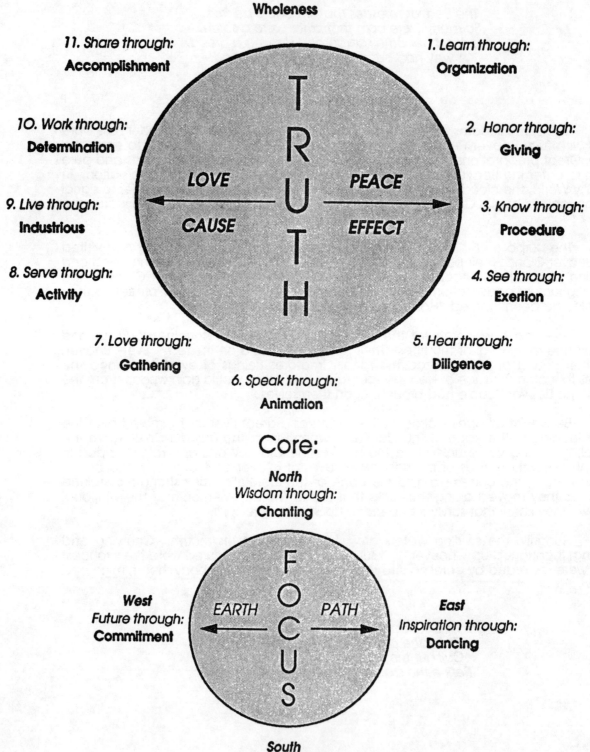

12. Thank through:
Wholeness

11. Share through:
Accomplishment

1. Learn through:
Organization

10. Work through:
Determination

2. Honor through:
Giving

LOVE   *PEACE*

9. Live through:
Industrious

3. Know through:
Procedure

CAUSE   *EFFECT*

8. Serve through:
Activity

4. See through:
Exertion

7. Love through:
Gathering

5. Hear through:
Diligence

6. Speak through:
Animation

T R U T H

Core:

North
Wisdom through:
Chanting

West
Future through:
Commitment

EARTH   *PATH*

East
Inspiration through:
Dancing

F O C U S

South
Lessons through:
Collecting

Bee
Decree of Perseverance

Stings do not happen just by chance,
For they occur at a glance.
Stings do induce a circumstance,
As the Bee's protesting lance.

In the beginning, when names were being given by the chief namer, a smaller member of the Flying Clans stood in line, waiting to be given their tasks to create the characteristics that resulted in their receiving a name.   One of the Ant People was heard as he spoke to another, "Everyone knows that Ant People are the finest workers. We expect a name that reflects our working nature."

A nearby Beaver over heard the conversation and thought, "I work continuously to find the proper trees to cut and to house my young. I am glad that I received a name like Beaver and not a name like She Who Works Hard.   All Creatures of Natureland certainly work to feed their young and teach them how to live."

A Bear who was teaching his Bear cub how to forage for food overheard the conversation and thought of the wonderful Honey Tree he had shown his young cub yesterday. He thought to himself, thinking no one was listening, "A good name for the honey maker would be..." but here, his thoughts were interrupted by a loud crash of Thunder and the Sky World lit up a with a brilliant lightning flash.

Listen all, Beings of Earth where Creatures dwell,
Hinoh listens as clear as a bell.
Thoughts come to me even while talking,
For days I've been thinking and stalking.

Names are not given just by chance,
Names often come during a dance.
Thoughts of Bear are true as can be,
A honey maker is a Bee.

Making Honey is their Sacred Job,
It's the gift of flowers they never rob.
Honey is food as pure as can be,
It can be found, stored, in a hallow tree.

From that time on, Bee buzzed its sound,
To let Clans know Bees where around.
Don't stop my work, honor the Bee,
Or stay away -- my stings are free.

Da Nahol

Buffalo

Contribution - Stamina

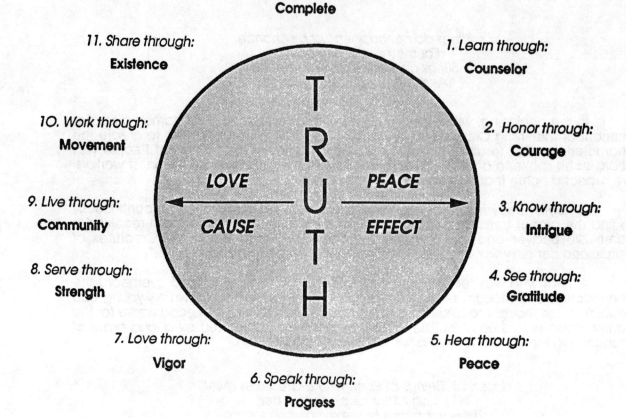

12. Thank through:
Complete

11. Share through:
Existence

1. Learn through:
Counselor

10. Work through:
Movement

2. Honor through:
Courage

LOVE · T R U T H · *PEACE*

CAUSE · *EFFECT*

9. Live through:
Community

3. Know through:
Intrigue

8. Serve through:
Strength

4. See through:
Gratitude

7. Love through:
Vigor

5. Hear through:
Peace

6. Speak through:
Progress

Core:

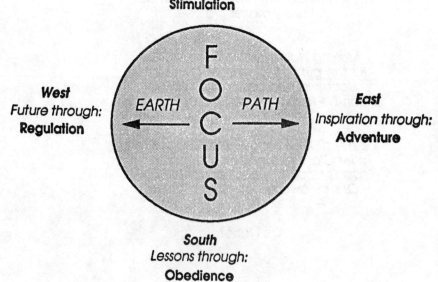

North
Wisdom through:
Stimulation

West
Future through:
Regulation

EARTH · F O C U S · *PATH*

East
Inspiration through:
Adventure

South
Lessons through:
Obedience

Buffalo
Decree of Stamina

On Turtle Island, life was abundant for all the Creature Beings who shared the gifts of Motherearth. However, survival gradually became a struggle as living grew into a daily task.

"What is happening to us?" asked the Buffalo. "Food is becoming more scarce each passing day. Let's send our Scouts to other Clans and see if they are having the same difficulties we are experiencing."

Two Buffalo Scouts volunteered to visit the North, where the climate was cold. Two Buffalo Scouts volunteered to scan the East to see if the same food shortage had spread in that direction. Two Buffalo Scouts traveled to the South in search for answers to their questions. Two Buffalo Scouts journeyed to the West to cast their eyes on the living conditions of their Western relatives.

When the eight seekers returned, they reported that food shortages and lodging places were scarce everywhere. A great Council was held to discuss what the future held in store for the living. During the height of the discussion, Grandfather Sun beat down on the Council of Buffalo. The heat was so intense that the Woodlands burst into fire. The Buffalo scurried to the lake to escape the scorching flames where they stood in reverent silence.

Suddenly, through the smoky clouds, Hinoh, the Thunder Chief, spoke:

A scourge of lust has descended upon us,
Your coats of fur are needed.
Your bodies are left to rot into mush,
With future growth unheeded.

Selfishness stops all gracious giving,
Lacks control and limits all living.
Life, once abundant, has taught self-survival,
Love must seed our Earth's revival.

Lives that have been shall be sacrificed,
As future growth is labeled and priced.
Yet fear not when, for now and then,
Earth laws shall restore what has been.

From this message, the Buffalo knew lean times would prevail. However, their kind would survive if they practiced Sacred Trust as their Wisdom and Gratitude.

Praise and abundance, Buffalo Wisdom serves wholly of itself to obtain oneness with all things. The Buffalo is the most secret of all animals, giving 100% of themselves not only for food but spiritually. Dream of the White Buffalo means the coming of abundance.

Cleansing Prevails, renews and restores,
Challenges precede as thought implores.
Life abundant awakens the hoard,
Seek withinness is where Peace is stored.

Da Naho!

Butterfly

Contribution - Beauty

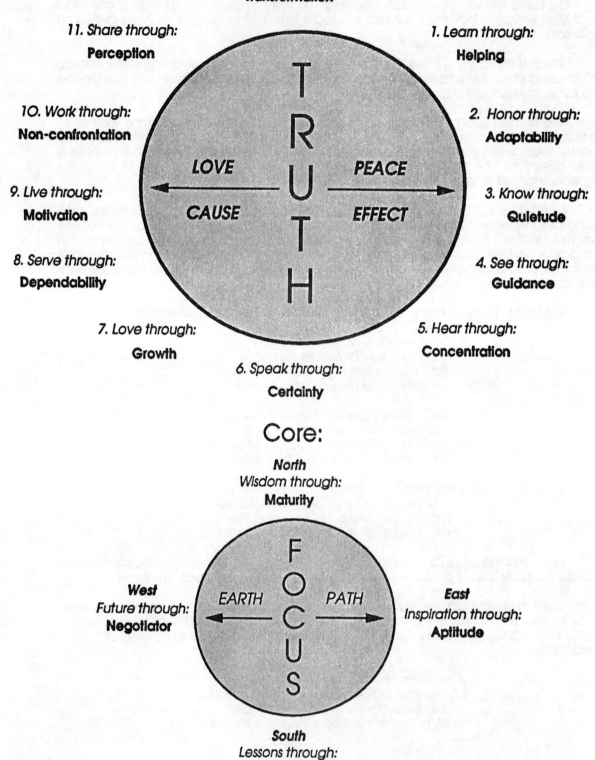

12. Thank through:
Transformation

11. Share through:
Perception

1. Learn through:
Helping

10. Work through:
Non-confrontation

2. Honor through:
Adaptability

LOVE   PEACE

9. Live through:
Motivation

CAUSE   EFFECT

3. Know through:
Quietude

8. Serve through:
Dependability

4. See through:
Guidance

7. Love through:
Growth

5. Hear through:
Concentration

6. Speak through:
Certainty

Core:

North
Wisdom through:
Maturity

West
Future through:
Negotiator

EARTH   PATH

East
Inspiration through:
Aptitude

South
Lessons through:
Patient

Butterfly
Decree of Beauty

The Gift of Beauty scribes imagination,
Transforming an image into fascination.
Perception encourages justification,
Confidence interprets the manifestation.

Many years ago, two charming Creature Crawlers feared they would be separated. To make sure this didn't happen, they secured themselves in a thread-like blanket called a cocoon and attached it to a twig of a tree. When the winds blew, the tree danced and rocked the two charming Creatures into the breeze.

"What a wonderful life we have," remarked one. "I'm getting bored because there is nothing to do," said the other. "Besides it's getting very warm. I think I'll peek out and see why there is so much heat."

So the bored Creature Crawler gently opened his thread-like blanket to see what was happening all around him. What he saw gave him a start. "Quick, leave the covering behind! A fire is eating the trees!" he shouted to the other Creature Crawler.

At that moment, the fire, with its bright color stick touched the blanket and changed the charming Creature Crawlers into Butterflies. From that day, Butterflies give Beauty to the Earth Environment.

Butterfly, Butterfly, where have you been?
Butterfly, Butterfly, you're light and trim.
Butterfly, Butterfly, light as a cloud,
Butterfly, Butterfly, charming and proud.

Transformation is related to the air moving through its currents. Getting into the flow of time and action. Butterfly Wisdom means spirit movement, from an immovable state to a movable state. Butterfly Wisdom gives a direction for change. The cocoon stage of its Sacred Space, made of the threads of life with its web to create its future. The state of being before transformation knows the time of change to invite beauty and charm.

The gift of enchantment,
Creates the advancement.
Transformation is a must,
Completion seals the trust.

Da Naho!

Chicken

Contribution -Sociability

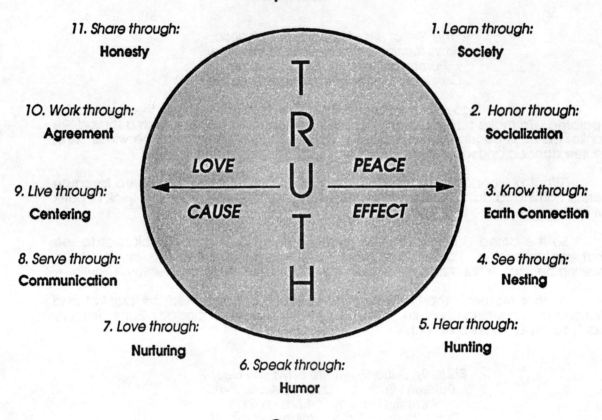

12. Thank through:
Preparation

11. Share through:
Honesty

1. Learn through:
Society

10. Work through:
Agreement

2. Honor through:
Socialization

LOVE   *PEACE*

T R U T H

CAUSE   *EFFECT*

9. Live through:
Centering

3. Know through:
Earth Connection

8. Serve through:
Communication

4. See through:
Nesting

7. Love through:
Nurturing

5. Hear through:
Hunting

6. Speak through:
Humor

Core:

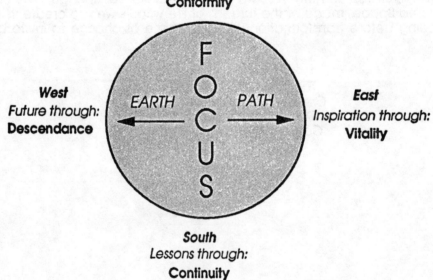

North
Wisdom through:
Conformity

West
Future through:
Descendance

EARTH   F O C U S   *PATH*

East
Inspiration through:
Vitality

South
Lessons through:
Continuity

Chicken

Decree of Sociability

When Chicken became a feathered breed,
Sacred Trusting sanctified their creed.
Nesting nurtures honesty,
Friendship loves community.

When Chicken emerged from Motherearth, they were naked and cold. Therefore, they huddled together to keep their bodies warm. Their gentle touching created a bond of togetherness. When Chicken began to look around they saw other Creature Beings who wore soft blankets to keep them warm. They asked some of these Creatures where they found their blankets.

"We eat the Cloud seeds when they visit the Earth," Chicken was told.

Day after day after day Chicken looked for the Cloud with seeds to visit the Earth. One day, without warning, a Cloud heavily laden with seeds enveloped them. Hungrily, Chicken ate every seed and sprouted the gift of feathers. Chicken attempted to fly like the other Feathered Beings but they were too heavy. The Cloud said:

Chicken, Chicken heaviest of all,
Is likened to a feathered ball.
Eating is a Chicken's daily chore,
And shall be eaten forevermore.

To this day, Chicken eats to be eaten. It has been said that Chicken transforms food into love.

Da Naho!

Cow

Contribution -Solemnity

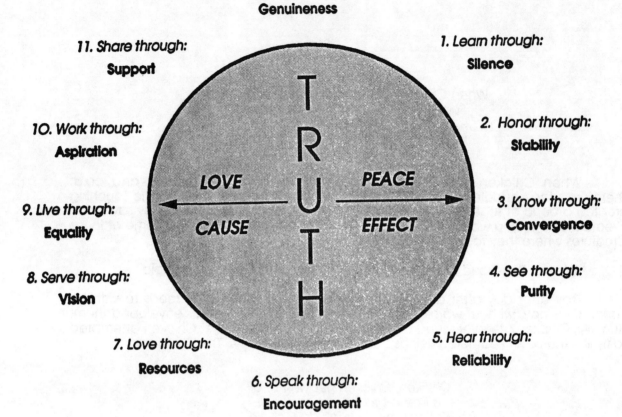

12. Thank through:
Genuineness

11. Share through:
Support

1. Learn through:
Silence

10. Work through:
Aspiration

2. Honor through:
Stability

9. Live through:
Equality

3. Know through:
Convergence

8. Serve through:
Vision

4. See through:
Purity

7. Love through:
Resources

5. Hear through:
Reliability

6. Speak through:
Encouragement

LOVE — **TRUTH** — *PEACE*
CAUSE — *EFFECT*

Core:

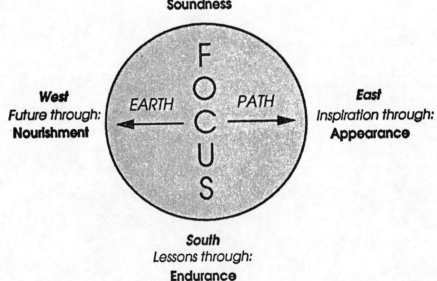

North
Wisdom through:
Soundness

West
Future through:
Nourishment

East
Inspiration through:
Appearance

South
Lessons through:
Endurance

EARTH — **FOCUS** — *PATH*

Cow
Decree of Solemnity

It makes no difference the size of the head
So long as there's stability.
The Ancient Ancestors have wisely said,
Wisdom is in the ability.

While the Motherearth was cooling and her Creatures were emerging into being, the spirit of Cows hovered in space looking for a physical image. The spirit of Cow possessed enormous eyes thus being visionaries was one of their gifts. When the physical body stood upright on Earth, it expressed a sturdy form.

Strength nurtures a worthy form,
Resourcefulness is the norm.
The Cow accepts a mission,
Its eyes foresee the vision.

These thoughts were encoded in the heart of the Cow. One after another they gathered to form a stable Clan. Their minds were not idle yet their vision was clouded. They stood in a circle with all heads facing the center. This position caused them to grow into bulky masses. They found themselves unable to turn from this position. They knew not how to back away from their circle. Therefore, they slowly pushed forward and reduced the size of the heads which bulged out their eyes. However, the movement of the Earth gave sense awareness to their bodies. To this day, Cows can move and twitch their skin due to their sensitivity to touch. Because of their gift of sensitivity, Cows became aware of the needs of other Creatures.

Two young children were lost in the Forestland and were tired and hungry. They came upon a herd of Cows and saw a Snake wrapped around the leg of one of them eating from the nipples that hung from the Cow's belly. After the Snake appeared full, it dropped to the ground and slithered away. The beautiful eye of the Cow invited the children to pull at her nipples. When they did this a white liquid streamed forth and the children sprayed it into their mouths. This Gift from the Cow kept them alive. When they were found at last, they told their people what had happened. From that time on, Cows became special friends of the People.

Da Naho!

Coyote

Contribution -Humor

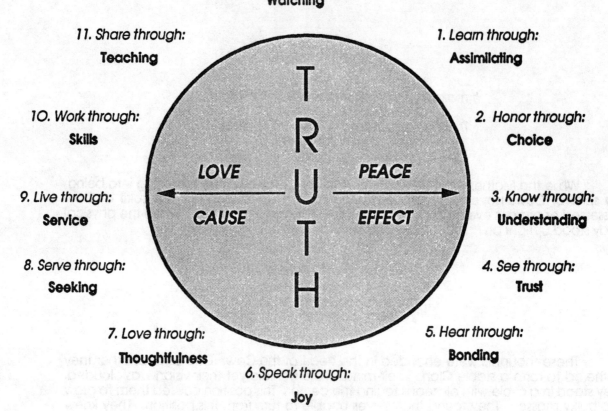

12. *Thank through:*
Watching

11. *Share through:*
Teaching

1. *Learn through:*
Assimilating

10. *Work through:*
Skills

2. *Honor through:*
Choice

LOVE   **TRUTH**   *PEACE*

CAUSE   *EFFECT*

9. *Live through:*
Service

3. *Know through:*
Understanding

8. *Serve through:*
Seeking

4. *See through:*
Trust

7. *Love through:*
Thoughtfulness

5. *Hear through:*
Bonding

6. *Speak through:*
Joy

Core:

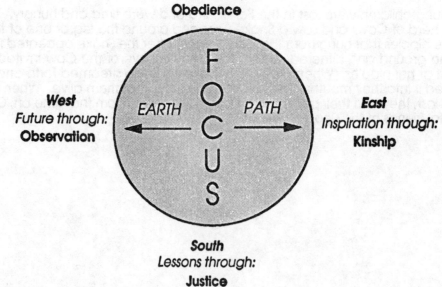

North
Wisdom through:
Obedience

West
Future through:
Observation

EARTH   **FOCUS**   *PATH*

East
Inspiration through:
Kinship

South
Lessons through:
Justice

Coyote
Decree of Humor

Coyote, Coyote come this way
There are lessons of truth to be learned each day.
When want seeks need, then want goes astray
When want becomes need, then need is fair play.

When the World was very young and Creature Beings were adjusting to the Earthmother's nature, Coyote left his pack to forage for himself. He found it strange that other Four-Leggeds didn't do the same. Sometimes Coyote thought being alone had its advantages and other times, he felt sad. However, there was one time that Coyote will never forget.

He had been resting under a bush during the heat of the day when a Mouse person appeared at the corner of his eye. A quick turn of his head and Mouse wasn't there.

"Come and follow me friend to the place of no end," Coyote heard in his ears.

"I must be hearing things," he thought and curled round and round, moving clockwise and cuddled to the ground.

Just as Coyote was about to fall asleep he heard, "Come follow me friend, to the place of no end." Again he thought he saw a Mouse at the corner of his eye. He jumped up for a second time, looked around, and saw no one. Each time Coyote cuddled close to the Earth he heard this strange Mouse voice.

Coyote was getting very tired for he was not getting his customary rest. The same procedure occurred throughout the day and well into the night until Coyote was very, very tired. Suddenly, Grandmother Moon lit the night Sky World, again Mouse spoke:

"Wake up Coyote friend!
Follow me to the place of no end."

Coyote leaped to his feet and followed what he thought was the same Mouse causing Coyote to dart from one direction into another. To this day, when Coyote sees Mouse out of the corner of his eye he has an urge to follow Mouse to the "place of no end."

Coyote, Coyote, come this way,
There are lessons of truth to learn each day.
Want seeks need - truth is fair play,
Thoughts welcome needs, then want goes astray.

Da Naho!

Crow

Contribution -Earth Law

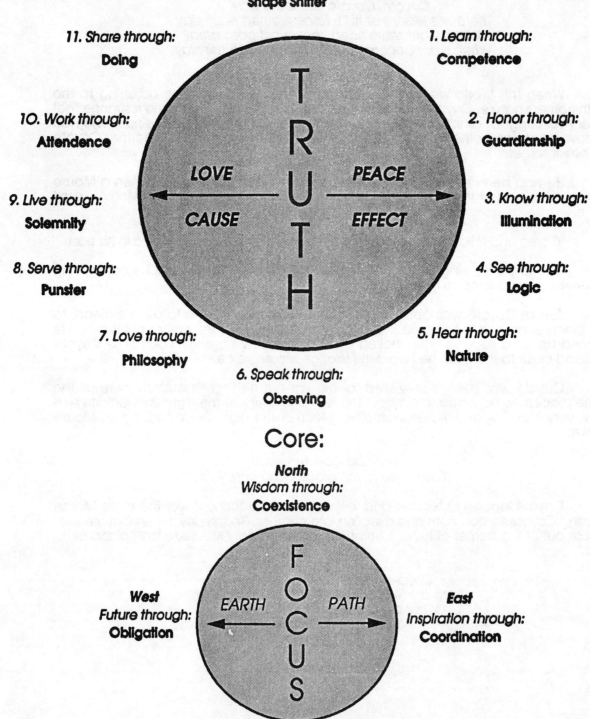

12. Thank through:
Shape Shifter

11. Share through:
Doing

1. Learn through:
Competence

10. Work through:
Attendence

2. Honor through:
Guardianship

LOVE *PEACE*

CAUSE *EFFECT*

9. Live through:
Solemnity

3. Know through:
Illumination

8. Serve through:
Punster

4. See through:
Logic

7. Love through:
Philosophy

5. Hear through:
Nature

6. Speak through:
Observing

Core:

North
Wisdom through:
Coexistence

West
Future through:
Obligation

EARTH *PATH*

East
Inspiration through:
Coordination

South
Lessons through:
Symbolic

Crow
Decree of Earth Law

While deep within the within, within,
There is a law of remembering.
That Love is the true Centering Light,
Serving all Peace as a Grounding Rite.

Many Moons ago, Crows attended a Council where the Wingeds received a Decree. When the Crow Clan entered the Council, they demonstrated their flight patterns and voiced their natural needs.

All the Feathered People listened, however, amid the Crow calls and flapping wings the minds of the Council members couldn't hear what the Crow was saying. As a result, the members of the Council became restless and an uproar filled the air. The Crows saw what was happening. To gain attention of the crowd, each Crow lifted its body into the air and suddenly dropped down to the Earth. This dramatic movement quieted the uproar and a great silence made everyone feel "whole".

A White Cloud descended from the Sky World and whispered:

Voices echo Peace around the world,
The reason for living must unfurl.
Crow is repeating in every Caw,
To touch the Earth is Sacred Law.

Da Naho!

Deer

Contribution -Skills

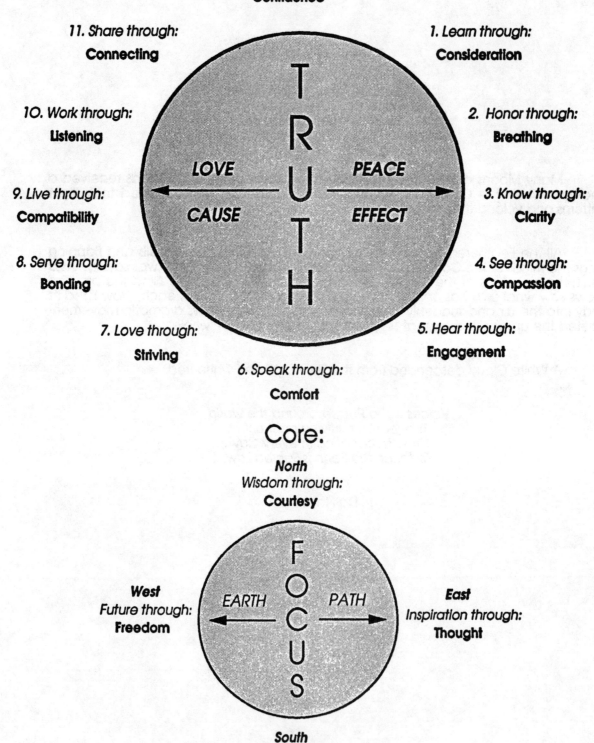

12. Thank through:
Confidence

11. Share through:
Connecting

1. Learn through:
Consideration

10. Work through:
Listening

2. Honor through:
Breathing

LOVE *PEACE*

T R U T H

CAUSE *EFFECT*

9. Live through:
Compatibility

3. Know through:
Clarity

8. Serve through:
Bonding

4. See through:
Compassion

7. Love through:
Striving

5. Hear through:
Engagement

6. Speak through:
Comfort

Core:

North
Wisdom through:
Courtesy

F O C U S

West
Future through:
Freedom

EARTH *PATH*

East
Inspiration through:
Thought

South
Lessons through:
Operation

Deer
Decree of Skills

In a deep forest lived many Deer. They were known to be gentle and non-aggressive. One day while four young Braves were tracking for small game, they heard a strange, rumbling sound. Spurred by their curiosity, it led them to seek the cause. Between the trees they saw a dust cloud. When they neared the dust cloud, a thundering sound reached their ears. They hurried their steps.

Suddenly before their eyes was the tallest Deer they had ever seen. The sight left them spellbound. "Let's kill that Deer to feed our People," said one of the Braves. Encouraged by the suggestion, the trackers silently crept toward their goal. Each one arched his bow, aimed, and sent a death weapon; but the arrows made no impression on the Great Deer.

Time and again they shot their arrows, yet the Deer stood unharmed. After spending all their weapons, they were disappointed in their failure to kill the Deer. Tired and downhearted they slumped against the trees. Soon sleep entered their bodies. Presently in their dreams, the Great Deer appeared and spoke to them:

I am Deerfoot the Great Runner,
I'm the Eldest, there's no other.
There are new skills you may earn,
Practice breathing you must learn.
Timing is the future's presence,
Join us in this timeless Essence.

Deerfoot has spoken.

Startled by the Deer's message, the Braves awakened to see that Deerfoot had come for them. Obediently they joined the Deer, and learned how to breathe while running.

These four Braves became the first runners, who carried messages from one village to the next, creating a network of communication. They learned that clarity in mind and conservation in body produced sensitivity and physical stamina. A Seneca named Deerfoot became known for this running skill. His home can be visited on the Cattaraugus Reservation, home of the Senecas.

Da Naho!

Dog
Contribution -Faithfulness

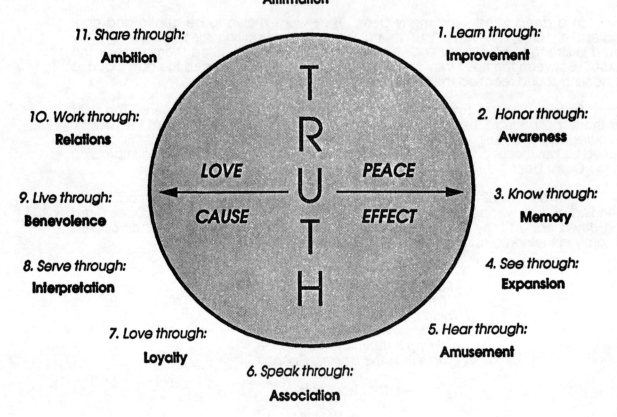

12. Thank through:
Affirmation

11. Share through:
Ambition

1. Learn through:
Improvement

10. Work through:
Relations

2. Honor through:
Awareness

LOVE   *PEACE*

T
R
U
T
H

CAUSE   *EFFECT*

9. Live through:
Benevolence

3. Know through:
Memory

8. Serve through:
Interpretation

4. See through:
Expansion

7. Love through:
Loyalty

5. Hear through:
Amusement

6. Speak through:
Association

Core:

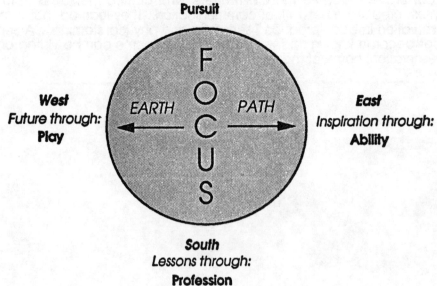

North
Wisdom through:
Pursuit

West
Future through:
Play

EARTH   *PATH*

F
O
C
U
S

East
Inspiration through:
Ability

South
Lessons through:
Profession

Dog
Decree of Loyalty

Loyalty comes from within the within,
Cycling Sacred Space at the outer rim.
Truth interacts with each emotion,
Accepting Love through Life's devotion.

There came a time in the growth of the Four-Leggeds that Dogs emerged as descendants of the Wolves.

Living was spiraling to the four directions,
Creatures were mirrors of inner reflections.
Earthlings in related cases,
Expanded images that formed new races.

The Wolves remained the source of the breed,
As the foundation proclaimed the need,
Countless new species began to emerge,
To satisfy growth as an inner urge.

Dogs became friends to walk on Earth,
And devoted their lives grounding their worth.
Thank the Great Mystery for serving the need,
As Motherearth sanctioned her loyalty creed.

What shall we call them? Entered each thought.
Canine was the name their breed begot.
Different sizes their bodies took form,
Suiting the need, Guardians were born.

Loyalty, dogs begot and served as brothers.
Fathers sired Mothers birthing all others.
The time came for Canines to foster new breeds
That they might protect all future human needs.

Da Naho!

Dolphin

Contribution -Clarity

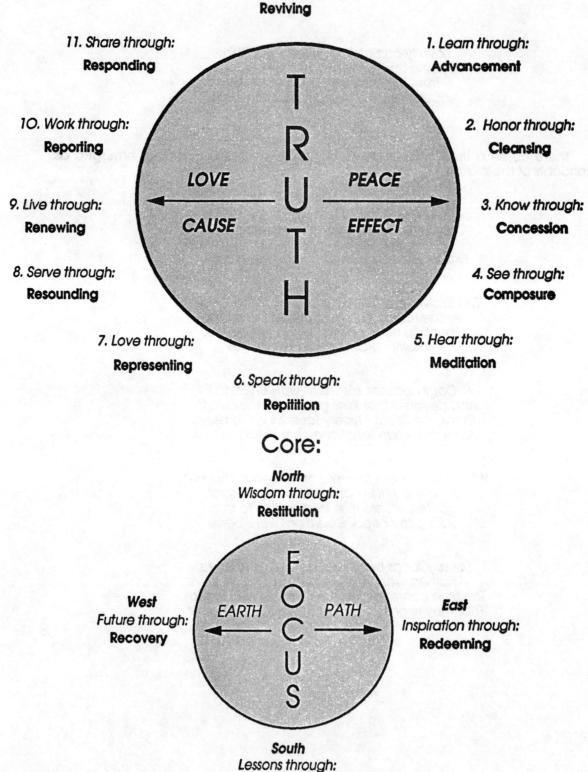

12. Thank through:
Reviving

11. Share through:
Responding

1. Learn through:
Advancement

10. Work through:
Reporting

2. Honor through:
Cleansing

LOVE T R U T H *PEACE*

CAUSE *EFFECT*

9. Live through:
Renewing

3. Know through:
Concession

8. Serve through:
Resounding

4. See through:
Composure

7. Love through:
Representing

5. Hear through:
Meditation

6. Speak through:
Repitition

Core:

North
Wisdom through:
Restitution

West
Future through:
Recovery

EARTH F O C U S *PATH*

East
Inspiration through:
Redeeming

South
Lessons through:
Refining

Dolphin
Decree of Clarity

As a gift of Peace each loving day
Freedom of movement provides the way.
Life abundant shall always know
Breathing creates the presence to grow.

In the beginning, all Creature Beings lived and grew with the Water Spirits. Life was abundant and growth was unlimited. Due to the unlimited growth, Creature Beings were expanding their forms, and taking up greater space. The phenomenal growth of the Creature Beings caused space to become crowded. As a result, the Creature Beings were experiencing a new feeling that produced stress – a lack of space in which to grow and limitation of their freedom to breathe.

Dolphin had received a gift that teaching was perceived as a lesson. The surrounding light had become clouded, as a result of overcrowding of all living forms. A voice from within spoke to Dolphin.

When Clarity is dulled within the mind,
Creating Space can awaken the blind.
That Freedom of movement might prevail,
Breathing in the sights that remove the veil.

Dolphin inhaled a deep breath, and while exhaling, its body was propelled into a clearing, that revealed an opening wide enough for all the Finned ones to enter and grow. To this day, Dolphin has been the Keeper of Sacred Breath, that Water Creatures use as their Essence of Clarity.

Da Naho!

Dragonfly

Contribution -Illumination

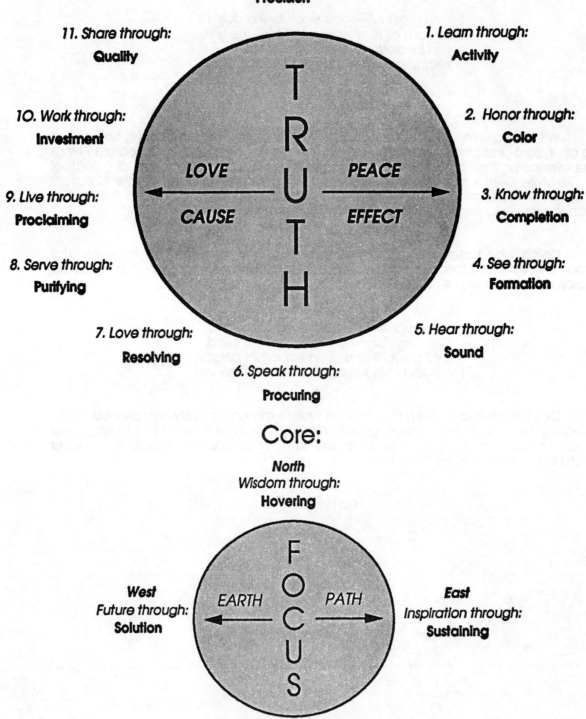

12. Thank through:
Precision

11. Share through:
Quality

1. Learn through:
Activity

10. Work through:
Investment

2. Honor through:
Color

LOVE

TRUTH

PEACE

9. Live through:
Proclaiming

CAUSE

EFFECT

3. Know through:
Completion

8. Serve through:
Purifying

4. See through:
Formation

7. Love through:
Resolving

5. Hear through:
Sound

6. Speak through:
Procuring

Core:

North
Wisdom through:
Hovering

West
Future through:
Solution

EARTH

FOCUS

PATH

East
Inspiration through:
Sustaining

South
Lessons through:
Practice

Dragonfly
Decree of Illumination

Truth has the criteria that credits its form
Peace is the apex existing within its norm
Illumination awakens inner vision
By creating the focus upon one's mission

Dragonfly did not always have its present form. Although it had four wings, they did not function as they do now. Dragonfly could enter any dimension of speed, as a situation occurred. This gift served their species well, until a situation became a condition.

At a Council of Insects, great stress was encountered, due to the expanded growth of Feathered Clans. The Feathered Clans were eating them faster than the Insect Clans could reproduce. If this situation continued, the health condition of the Forest Clans would be jeopardized.

Dragonfly entered the Silence and received the following vision.

Dragonfly, Dragonfly, stall your condition,
Secure your wings in a firmed position.

"How can I do this?" asked Dragonfly.

"Your Truth Line is forthright, your wings become firm.
Love, Truth and Peace, cause and effect you may earn."

From that time, Dragonfly's body symbolized Trust through stability. The two upper wings symbolize Love and Peace, the two lower wings symbolize Cause and Effect. Love must flow through Truth to have Peace. Cause must flow through Truth to have a good Effect.

Da Naho!

Eagle

Contribution -Ideals

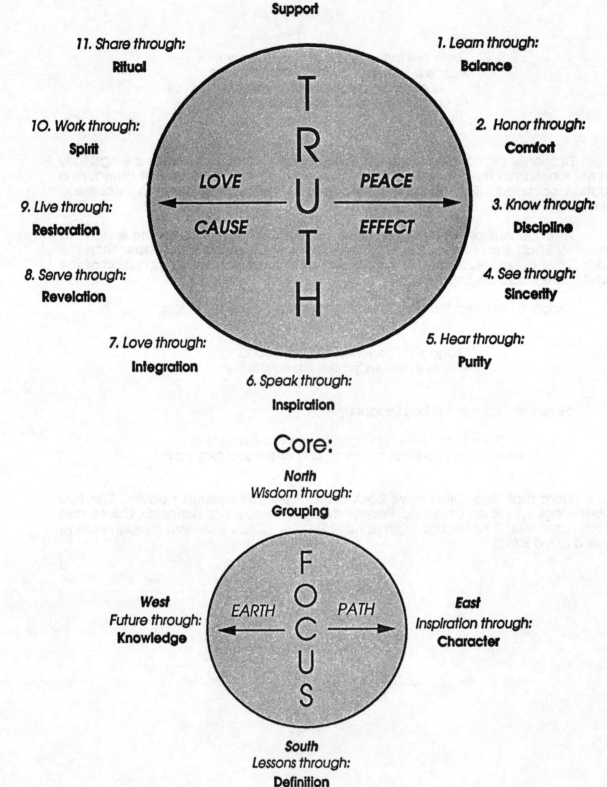

12. *Thank through:*
Support

11. *Share through:*
Ritual

1. *Learn through:*
Balance

10. *Work through:*
Spirit

2. *Honor through:*
Comfort

LOVE — PEACE

9. *Live through:*
Restoration

CAUSE — EFFECT

3. *Know through:*
Discipline

T R U T H

8. *Serve through:*
Revelation

4. *See through:*
Sincerity

7. *Love through:*
Integration

5. *Hear through:*
Purity

6. *Speak through:*
Inspiration

Core:

North
Wisdom through:
Grouping

F O C U S

West
Future through:
Knowledge

EARTH — PATH

East
Inspiration through:
Character

South
Lessons through:
Definition

Eagle
Decree of Peace

Many Moons ago, when the Wingeds accepted their lives and purposes, Eagle was given a message.

Eagle, Eagle, soaring high,
Sacred Speaker of the Sky.
Inspired integrity, harmony spiraling,
Oh! Gracious Eagle, heightens inspiring.

The Mystery is life unending,
The Mystery is purpose blending.
The Mystery is seen descending,
The Mystery is knowledge transcending.

But why do I hear this strange sound?
Your message interprets Sacred Ground.
Eagle listened, for from this withinness,
Every sound has its natural beginness.

Eagle flew around countless suns,
Life would be varied for winged ones.
But soon a Decree would weave its way,
As the Rainbow of Peace brightened each day.

Earthmother beckoned to this Winged Ancestor,
Setting a forum to guide the adventure.
The Cycle of Truth would generate easement,
Growth would be fruitful without appeasement.

Councils were formed throughout Natureland,
With chiefs to represent each Winged Clan.
Breeding would secure freedom from blight,
As Winged ones chose their Sacred Rite.

Eagle became the Messenger of Peace
Countless moons this message would release.
Eagle soars into the endless sky
A symbol of Peace, no one can deny.

Da Naho!

Elk

Contribution -Balance

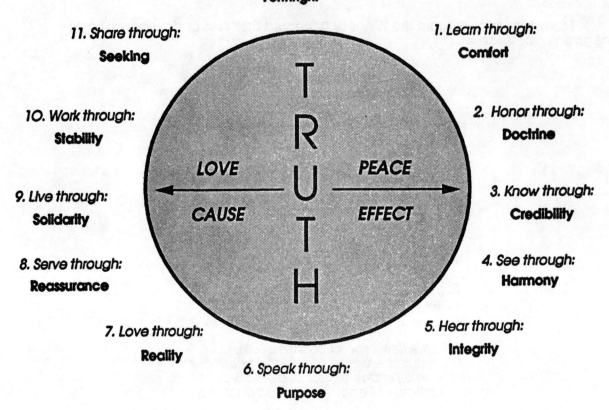

12. Thank through:
Forthright

11. Share through:
Seeking

1. Learn through:
Comfort

10. Work through:
Stability

2. Honor through:
Doctrine

LOVE   **PEACE**

TRUTH

CAUSE   **EFFECT**

9. Live through:
Solidarity

3. Know through:
Credibility

8. Serve through:
Reassurance

4. See through:
Harmony

7. Love through:
Reality

5. Hear through:
Integrity

6. Speak through:
Purpose

Core:

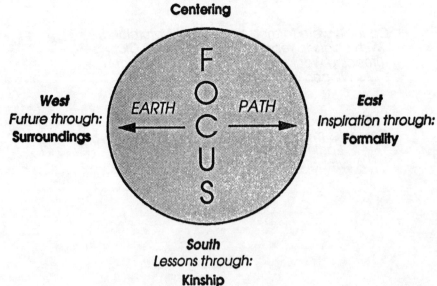

North
Wisdom through:
Centering

West
Future through:
Surroundings

EARTH   **PATH**

FOCUS

East
Inspiration through:
Formality

South
Lessons through:
Kinship

Elk
Decree of Balance

While growing is attuning the knowledge of talents,
Unfolding the gifts to create a balance.
Elk's bonding within a creed was born.
Enhances an image to fulfill its Earth Form.

The Elk is a large member of the Deer family, with an extension of Deer gifts of birth. An Elk experience unfolds in this legend. An Elk family lived in an ideal place. Their lifestyle was complete with ample foods and lodging places. It happened that an Elder Elk sensed a great storm on its way that might trap many many Forest Creatures who lived near the lake. Days before the storm, the Elder Elk had received its approaching signals.

The Elk directed the Forest Creatures to congregate at the lake. The Creatures stacked food in safe places, wedged between rocks. A gentle breeze sang through the trees where the Creatures had assembled.

The old Elk spoke to his family and kin,
And told of his hearing and vision within.
Feel the air currents glide between the trees,
Whistling their messages along with the breeze.

Tell all Creatures to harken their listening,
Lead them to safety where water lies glistening.
Tell them to stand with heads above water,
So they will look much like an Otter.

Then came a strong wind with hot lightening flashes,
It ignited the leaves and tall dry grasses.
The flames lit the trees and cindered the branches,
Leaving them to stand like Peace Warrior lances.

After the hot air had cindered all places,
The Creatures Beings praised their safe air spaces.
They emerged from where the water was tame,
And began to learn how to survive with acclaim.

Hinoh, the Thunderer spoke.

New growth will appear after the burnout,
As Nature takes care of all fear and doubt.
Creature Beings share your skills and talents,
For you have received the Decree of Balance.

Hinoh, has spoken.

Da naho!

Fox

Contribution -Withinness

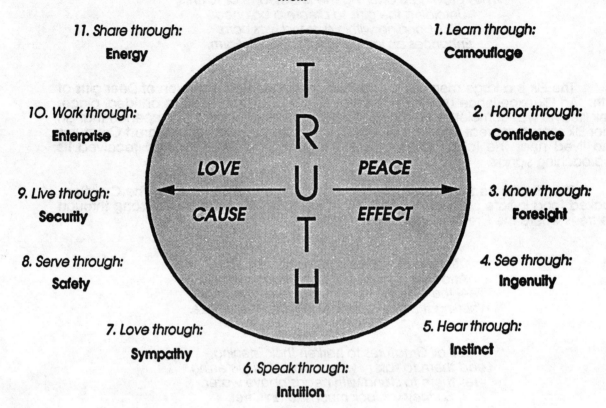

12. Thank through:
Merit

11. Share through:
Energy

1. Learn through:
Camouflage

10. Work through:
Enterprise

2. Honor through:
Confidence

9. Live through:
Security

3. Know through:
Foresight

8. Serve through:
Safety

4. See through:
Ingenuity

7. Love through:
Sympathy

5. Hear through:
Instinct

6. Speak through:
Intuition

TRUTH
LOVE — *PEACE*
CAUSE — *EFFECT*

Core:

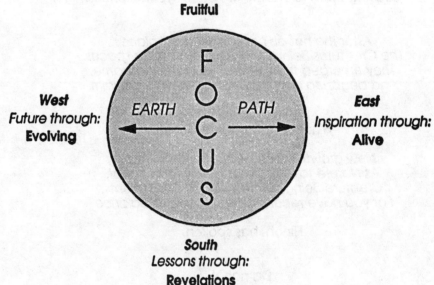

North
Wisdom through:
Fruitful

West
Future through:
Evolving

East
Inspiration through:
Alive

South
Lessons through:
Revelations

FOCUS
EARTH — *PATH*

Fox

Decree of Camouflage

Many Moons ago there lived a young, adventurous Fox who left his Clan to seek his wisdom. He knew that he was led by some Mysterious Force to earn his worth. When he was a short distance from his pack, he was startled by a large Porcupine. His body stiffened with fear.

"Take your fear," came a voice from within,
"You can learn about your centering."
Go to the North, then East, South and West,
Learn how camouflage can serve you best.

Fox felt uncomfortable as Porcupine spoke:

"Come! There's food galore of every kind,
Come! Or you'll be lost and left behind."
Fox followed Porcupine through the night,
Not a morsel of food was in sight.

They went to the North, then to the East,
Their hunger sought food for a feast.
South would provide a lesson for him,
He soon learned how to listen within.

Fox's last direction was to the West,
Time drew near for a well-earned rest.
Humbly he snuggled into Earth's care,
Where love had brought trust into his lair.

Now life was safe, self-confidence earned,
Return to your Clan, teach what you've learned.

Fox would never be the same as he headed back to his kin. The pack greeted him and:

They listened to his exciting tales,
And the gifts he earned from the teaching trails.
From that time on, Fox's wisdom could see,
That camouflaged spirits set them free.

Da Naho!

Frog

Contribution -Maturity

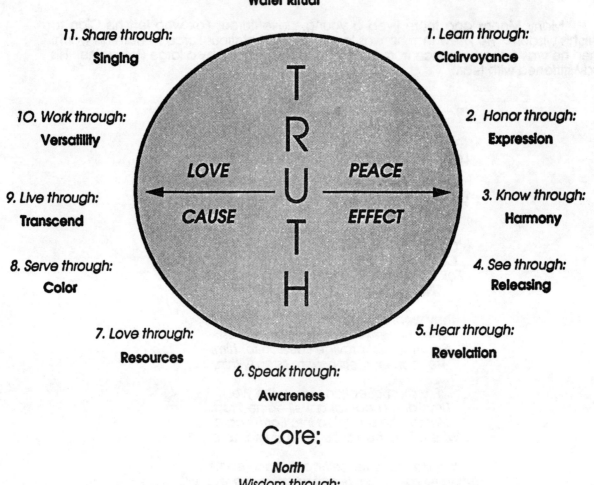

12. Thank through:
Water Ritual

11. Share through:
Singing

1. Learn through:
Clairvoyance

10. Work through:
Versatility

2. Honor through:
Expression

LOVE   PEACE

TRUTH

9. Live through:
Transcend

CAUSE   EFFECT

3. Know through:
Harmony

8. Serve through:
Color

4. See through:
Releasing

7. Love through:
Resources

5. Hear through:
Revelation

6. Speak through:
Awareness

Core:

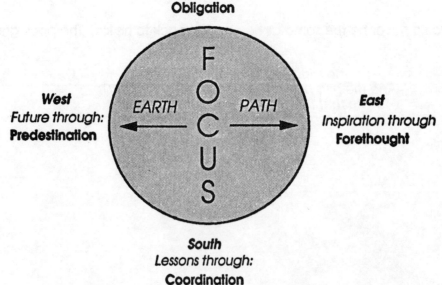

North
Wisdom through:
Obligation

West
Future through:
Predestination

EARTH   PATH

FOCUS

East
Inspiration through
Forethought

South
Lessons through:
Coordination

Frog
Decree of Maturity

When ideas form reality,
By developing clarity,
Seeds of truth start entering,
Harmony blends the centering.

Cleansing body, heart and mind,
Bonds life's spirit every time.
Change its legacy,
To guide growth maturity.

The two Frogs looked into each other's eyes,
For life had been clear without disguise.
Transforming change through development,
Made living secure accomplishment.

Singing harmonizes with the wind of choices,
Frogs can synthesize with resonating voices.

Two old Frogs, male and female, sat on a big lily pad reminiscing about their kin. "Life has been good to us," remarked the female. "Yes," agreed the male.

"Let's think about the time we were Tadpoles. What a challenge it was, to swim and hide from the beavers," added the female. "And remember what fun it was to sing each spring."

Tadpoles, Tadpoles, one and all,
Join the chorus, large and small.
Tadpoles, Tadpoles, we are free,
Singing with one family.
Toads and Frogs all come to croak,
Jump and swim beneath the Oak.

"Remember how strange it was to watch our forms change from Tadpoles to Frogs?"

We lived in the water,
Until spring awakening time.
We croak in the summer,
When we reached our prime.
Tadpoles, Toads, and Frogs - all are kin,
We can sing because we're tuned-in.

We learn our legacy of being Frogs.

Every day sees a change at play,
Growing, knowing, sharing life's way.
When ideas form reality,
To developing maturity.

Da Nahol

Goat

Contribution -Fulfillment

12. *Thank through:*
Nourishing

11. *Share through:*
Restfulness

1. *Learn through:*
Offering

10. *Work through:*
Patience

2. *Honor through:*
Coordinating

9. *Live through:*
Happiness

3. *Know through:*
Cooperating

8. *Serve through:*
Gladness

4. *See through:*
Clarity

7. *Love through:*
Faithfulness

5. *Hear through:*
Determination

6. *Speak through:*
Ease

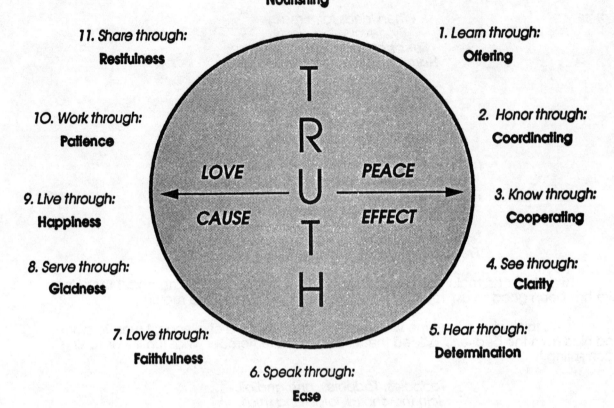

LOVE *PEACE*

CAUSE *EFFECT*

T R U T H

Core:

North
Wisdom through:
Categorize

West
Future through:
Consenting

EARTH *PATH*

F O C U S

East
Inspiration through:
Aesthetic

South
Lessons through:
Prescribing

Goat
Decree of Fulfillment

A long time ago, when Earth Creatures were just beginning to be aware that Grandmother Moon came back to the Earth's Sky World on a regular basis and most of Earth's Creatures had already formed their habits of life. Goat was the principle one for being different among those who had not yet submitted to having their life formed into harmony with others. Goat lived a style of life all his own. When the other grass eaters went out to eat, Goat lay down to rest and watch the others as they ate their fill of grass. When the others had filled their bellies, Goat felt hunger strike him and he jumped to his feet and rapidly ate grass wherever he could find it.

Grass was scarce for Goat, as the other Creatures had already cleaned up their part of the lush green grass. Goat voiced his displeasure with a loud voice and struggled on, here and there, eating the left over bits the others had not eaten. Goat soon learned to eat brush and bits of food that the others did not care for and Goat displayed a loud voice of disapproval.

Before many Moons had passed, Goat was wandering among the more ambitious Creatures who enjoyed their green grass. Goat was developing his lifelong habits at this time, and did not realize that the other Creatures preferred to eat their grass in silence and peace. Whenever Goat ate, his loud blasting voice made him unwanted. At a time when Creatures were learning to get along with each other in a peaceful manner, Goat was becoming more unwanted because of his belching, bleating and outrageous cry. Filled, the unhappy Goat laid down to sleep.

Hinoh, the Thunder Chief, passed by on his roads and took notice of the plight of the Goat. Hinoh spoke softly to his band of little rain clouds and told them to let their rain fall gently on Goat and other nearby Creatures. Rain fell on Goat and he woke up from his mid-day nap and gave his loud cry of anger. At that time, Hinoh was far off, but his voice came quietly to Goat and the others nearby heard the Decree:

Listen my friend, listen within--

Goat began to listen to his within,
He learned a nourishing gift he could win.
Rain from the sky will cleanse you from dust,
Your loud cry will be a signal of trust.

Goat had eaten what others had left
By living the way that served him best.
After Goat has lost what friendship meant
He learned how peace restored fulfillment.

Da Naho!

Grouse
Contribution -Dance

12. *Thank through:*
Visionary

11. *Share through:*
Teaching

1. *Learn through:*
Sufficient

10. *Work through:*
Ambition

2. *Honor through:*
Commitment

LOVE   **PEACE**

T R U T H

CAUSE   **EFFECT**

9. *Live through:*
Ritual

3. *Know through:*
Connectivity

8. *Serve through:*
Touching

4. *See through:*
Enthusiasm

7. *Love through:*
Movement

5. *Hear through:*
Experiencing

6. *Speak through:*
Imagination

Core:

North
Wisdom through:
Ascending

F O C U S

EARTH   **PATH**

West
Future through:
Obliging

East
Inspiration through:
Impression

South
Lessons through:
Bonding

Grouse
Decree of Dance

A state of harmony prevailed after Motherearth had provided food for all her Creature Beings. The Creature Beings were so busy exploring the abundance provided by their caretaker. Life was an expression of beauty. Soon, a feeling of discontentment began to appear. No one knew where it had its start, however here and there the feeling caused uneasiness among the Earth Dwellers.

Expressions of joy began to hide, sparkling eyes became dull. Beauty was replaced by impending fear. Happy Wingeds established a pecking game and stole from each other's nests. The time of abundance was scourged with a growing unrest.

The time had come, peace was nowhere
Healing had been a sad affair.
The Grouse was asked because they cared,
How to see beauty and repair.

When this responsibility was placed upon the Grouse, they had no idea what to do. While they sat in Council, a strong wind came from the North, lifted and spiraled them into the air. Soon their bodies spun into a dance, a beautiful revelation. After a time, the wind gently carried them back to the Earth.

The Grouse performed a movement that brought them an experience of Peace. When all the Creature Beings saw the dance of the Grouse, they were uplifted by the spiral movements.

Round and round the spiral advances
It's become the Sacred of Dances
It heals, restores enthusiasm
The Sacred Spiral Dance of Wisdom.

Grouse became the teachers of the Sacred Dancing Spiral that healed and restored and returned enthusiasm to the eyes of the Wingeds. To this day, Grouse performs the Dancing Spiral to reinforce their Peace.

Da Naho!

Hawk

Contribution -Respect

12. *Thank through:*
Truth

11. *Share through:*
Symbols

1. *Learn through:*
Change

10. *Work through:*
Situation

2. *Honor through:*
Decisions

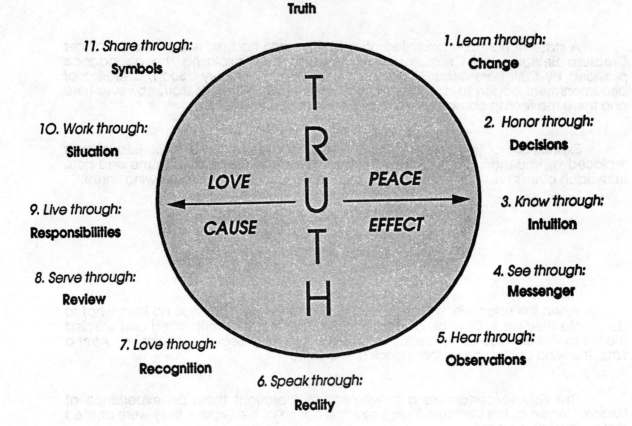

9. *Live through:*
Responsibilities

3. *Know through:*
Intuition

8. *Serve through:*
Review

4. *See through:*
Messenger

7. *Love through:*
Recognition

5. *Hear through:*
Observations

6. *Speak through:*
Reality

Core:

North
Wisdom through:
Partnership

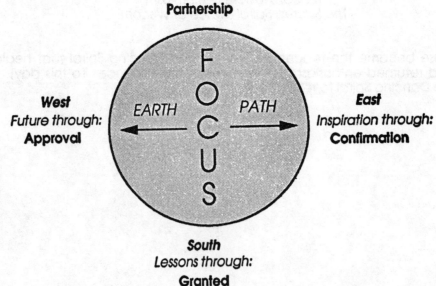

West
Future through:
Approval

East
Inspiration through:
Confirmation

South
Lessons through:
Granted

Hawk
Decree of Respect

Hawk and Eagle were honorable friends, and often carried messages for each other. Eagle was the cloud flying friend, while Hawk carried messages to the below Cloud People. It happened that Eagle saw the Two Leggeds wantonly destroying the Wingeds, whose work maintains the balance of all life.

A Council of Hawks and Eagles was held to alert the Two-Leggeds of their wrongdoing. It was decided that Hawk would approach a Two-Legged, who had boasted of his killing skill. The Hawk spoke.

Killing Creature Beings destroys the Sacred Web,
Know the precious workings that stabilizes the Ebb.
Life is amicable when Earthlings cease their tiffs,
Love, Truth and Peace births wholeness - partnerships share their gifts.

The Two-Legged dropped his head in shame,
He saw that his killing was to blame.

On that day, he accepted the Decree,
Respect for life preserves harmony.
Learn every action that Hawks portray,
For they protect travelers in a Sacred Way.

Da Naho!

Heron

Contribution -Fertilization

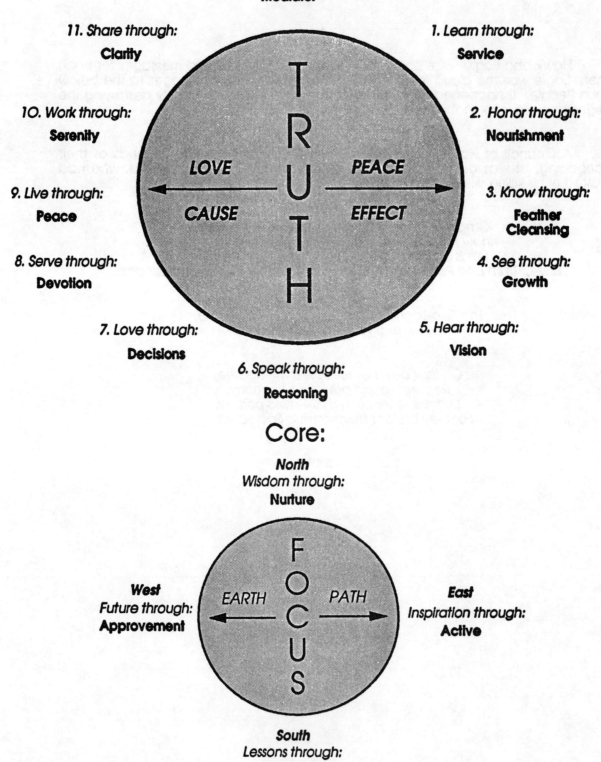

12. Thank through:
Mediator

11. Share through:
Clarity

1. Learn through:
Service

10. Work through:
Serenity

2. Honor through:
Nourishment

LOVE — PEACE

CAUSE — EFFECT

TRUTH

9. Live through:
Peace

3. Know through:
Feather Cleansing

8. Serve through:
Devotion

4. See through:
Growth

7. Love through:
Decisions

5. Hear through:
Vision

6. Speak through:
Reasoning

Core:

North
Wisdom through:
Nurture

West
Future through:
Approvement

East
Inspiration through:
Active

EARTH — PATH

FOCUS

South
Lessons through:
Wholeness

Heron

Decree of Fertilization

The tall, sturdy Blue Heron brought feelings of serenity into the places they lived. There was a time in Earth's growth that a lack of rain caused a shortage of food for all Creature Beings. Blue Heron recognized that a lesson was near for them to make a contribution to a new awakening.

Hinoh, the Thunder Chief, had not been feared by the Earthlings. It was time for the awakening. Hinoh announced:

Time makes a change in Sight Awareness
Time upholds faith in self-preparedness
Planting seeds for future growing
Reaps nourishment for inner-knowing

Hinoh's lightning rays invited the Rain People to dance upon Motherearth. The excited Raindrops swelled the waterways and flooded the land. Earthmother's thirst was satisfied, leaving Water Beings stranded along the shore. Countless Finneds were left to die. The following season, the plants that stood among the decayed life of the Creatures were taller, stronger, and denser in growth. Blue Heron then understood what the Finneds had contributed to their Inner-Knowing. They called a Council and entered the Dreamstate of every being, saying:

Fertilization enhances growing,
Life abundant welcomes Inner-Knowing.
Decaying matter produces balance,
That views the source of Nature's Talents.

At that moment, every Creature Being recognized that fertilization, both spiritual and physical, helped Motherearth reproduce her gifts.

Da Nahol

Horse

Contribution -Responsibility

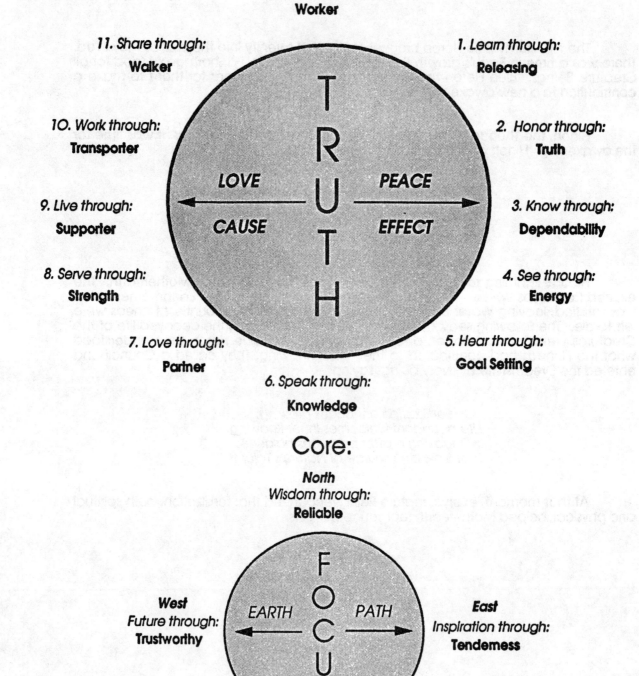

12. Thank through:
Worker

11. Share through:
Walker

1. Learn through:
Releasing

10. Work through:
Transporter

2. Honor through:
Truth

LOVE — TRUTH — PEACE

CAUSE — EFFECT

9. Live through:
Supporter

3. Know through:
Dependability

8. Serve through:
Strength

4. See through:
Energy

7. Love through:
Partner

5. Hear through:
Goal Setting

6. Speak through:
Knowledge

Core:

North
Wisdom through:
Reliable

FOCUS

West
Future through:
Trustworthy

EARTH — PATH

East
Inspiration through:
Tenderness

South
Lessons through:
Authentic

Horse
Decree of Responsibility

Horse had entered the Earth World as a being of strength and dependability. Horse possessed beauty and speed, yet would have to be directed.

Horse lived where space was unlimited, and grazing was abundant.   Thus, Horse became a social Creature where they depended upon each other to act as one. This feeling of unity prevented direction to develop. Horse was sensitive to Earth energy.   There came a time when Horse had increased their number to such a population, that grazing places were hard to find. They corralled in a box canyon for safety and security. Before long, the food was gone, and no leader was available to lead them out of the canyon. Hunger and confusion entered each Creature as they circled endlessly, lost in their dilemma.   Cloud People hovered over the canyon and knew Horse would soon secure a Decree. When Horse had entered the point of exhaustion, Hinoh, the Thunder Chief, roared and lightning flashed a resounding cadence.

Awaken to the Horse Decree,
Accept sensitivity, practice responsibility.
A leader shall appear, to guide you out of here,
You'll become a transporter, and a stalwart supporter.

Hinoh has spoken!

Thunder roared and lightning flashed to bring forth the apparition, suddenly, Thunder Wolf appeared to Horse and decreed their direction. As Thunder Wolf led the Horses out from the box canyon, they were met by the Two-Leggeds who were waiting for them. The Two-Leggeds mounted the Horses and to this day, Horse has been a friend and partner to Humankind. Mankind, the supporter of the Horse -- and Horse, the transporter of Man.

Direction became the need of Horse,
Who stands as a strong, able resource.
Beauty reveals a devoted steed,
Its gift is aiding a human's need.

Da Naho!

Hummingbird

Contribution -Energy

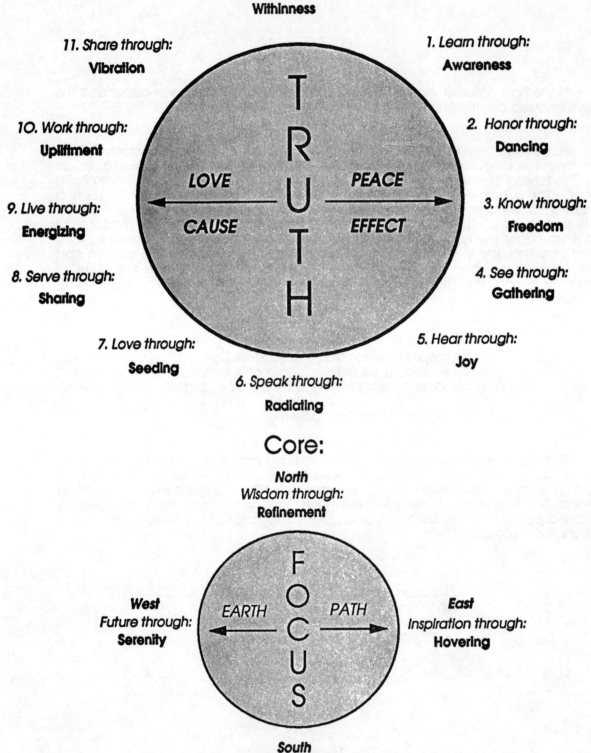

12. Thank through:
Withinness

11. Share through:
Vibration

1. Learn through:
Awareness

10. Work through:
Upliftment

2. Honor through:
Dancing

LOVE   PEACE

TRUTH

CAUSE   EFFECT

9. Live through:
Energizing

3. Know through:
Freedom

8. Serve through:
Sharing

4. See through:
Gathering

7. Love through:
Seeding

5. Hear through:
Joy

6. Speak through:
Radiating

Core:

North
Wisdom through:
Refinement

West
Future through:
Serenity

EARTH   PATH

FOCUS

East
Inspiration through:
Hovering

South
Lessons through:
Resourceful

Hummingbird
Decree of Energy

Many Suns ago, Hummingbird wished to fly with the Eagles into the Sky World. Everywhere Hummingbird went he told of his desire.

A time came when the desire became so great, the Hummingbirds decided to hold a Council, to make their desire come true. One of the Hummingbirds spoke.

"I talked with a Wren and told him of our desire to fly with Eagles in the Sky World. 'It's cold up there, the air is so rare,' warned the Wren.
"Then I talked with a Crow who said 'It's cold up there, the air is so rare, you can't see, nor can you breathe.
"Next, I talked with Hawk who reported, 'It's cold up there, the air is so rare you can't see, nor can you breathe. It's too high you'll surely die.'"

Yet, the Hummingbirds still wanted to fly with the Eagles in the Sun World.

When the rest of the Creatures heard the Hummingbirds wish, the Wingeds had created a chatter and their twittering had turned into laughter.

"Don't laugh at Hummingbird, his wishes have been heard," sang Eagle.

Hummingbird, Hummingbird, come to my side.
How would you like an Eagle ride?

"Nestle into my talons and I'll take you to my nest." Eagle carefully clutched Hummingbird in his talons and flew into the Sky World. Up, up, up they rose until Hummingbird no longer saw the Earth. Eagle flew up above the Cloud People, who surrounded his nest.

Eagle carefully placed his passenger among the Eaglets. "What food is this?" asked Eagle Wife. "A rare Hummingbird," responded Eagle Mate. The Eaglets looked at the rare Earth Creature in wonderment.

"It's time to leave while you're still alive," prompted the Eagle. Then, safely lifting Hummingbird from the nest, Eagle swooped and soared, during his descent to the Earth World, while the Council was still in session. Eagle announced:

Hummingbird, Hummingbird, now you have learned,
We just live in places we have earned.
When wishes are nebulous without form,
We make them worthy when we are born.

Eagle has spoken.

The time I spent in the Sun World was a find,
My wish to be a Hummingbird of the best kind.

From then, Hummingbirds are known to be swift,
To fly very fast has become their gift.
Suspending their energy is their quest,
The Hummingbird does this the very best.

Da Nahol

Lizard

Contribution -Memory

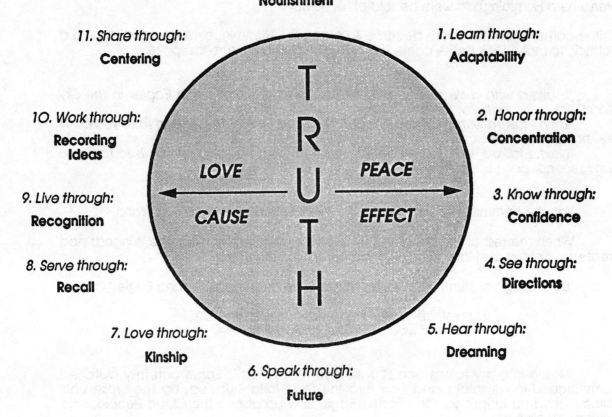

12. Thank through:
Nourishment

11. Share through:
Centering

1. Learn through:
Adaptability

10. Work through:
Recording Ideas

2. Honor through:
Concentration

LOVE **TRUTH** **PEACE**

CAUSE **EFFECT**

9. Live through:
Recognition

3. Know through:
Confidence

8. Serve through:
Recall

4. See through:
Directions

7. Love through:
Kinship

5. Hear through:
Dreaming

6. Speak through:
Future

Core:

North
Wisdom through:
Vision

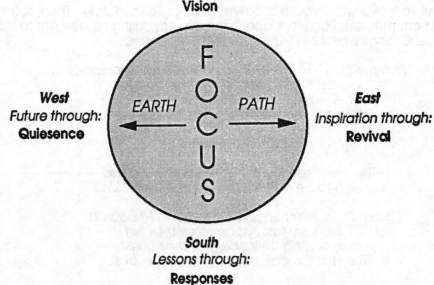

West
Future through:
Quiesence

FOCUS

EARTH **PATH**

East
Inspiration through:
Revival

South
Lessons through:
Responses

Lizard
Decree of Memory

Lizard is a dreamer and gifted with recall
They can enter Dreamtime and not be seen at all

In time long past, Lizard was not like the Lizard today. They lived among the rocks and hid close to the Earth. They were very lonesome Creature Beings. Lizards appeared like shadows, in dark lonely places.

"Oh, to be seen and loved," they wished. "Oh, to be a living dream. Oh, to be heard and sung about. Oh, to be useful and serene."

Motherearth heard this plea, for she loved them all. Perhaps a Decree can answer your wishes," she told them.   Gradually there eyes began to move independently, and they could look in every direction. Next their skin began to change color to match the surroundings.

It's time for you to enter the light,
And develop your dreams and insight.
When this happens, the gift of the Sun,
Will change your name to Chameleon.

Earth Mother has spoken!

Lizard became the Dream Seer and enlivened the Dreams of people to gift them with the Gift of Dream Recall. Lizards became the Chameleons and lived in the Sun's warmth, wherever human society allows.

People who live in places where Lizards are found can sit in the area because the environment is conducive to Peace.

Lizard, Lizard, the Dreamer of Peace,
Come as my friend that joy may increase.
Memories sweet, wait for more recall,
Please catch the enchantment, one and all.

Da Nahol

Lynx

Contribution -Logic

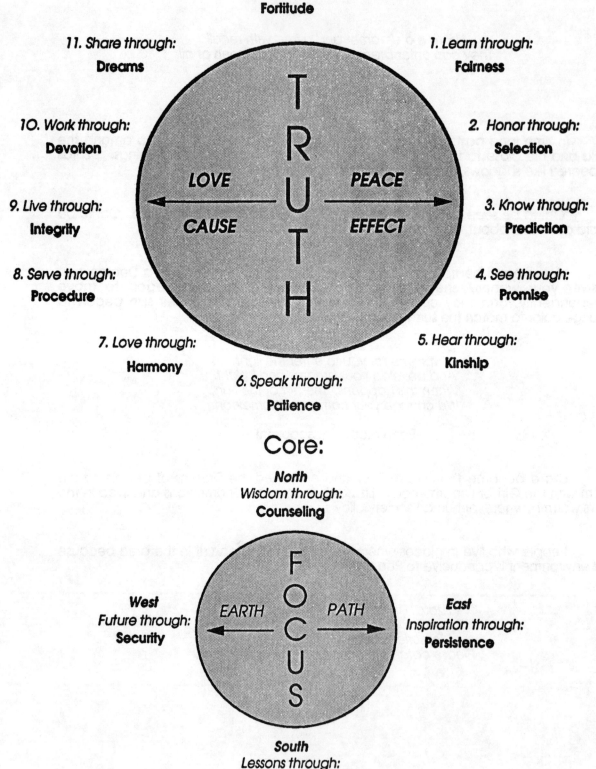

12. Thank through:
Fortitude

11. Share through:
Dreams

1. Learn through:
Fairness

10. Work through:
Devotion

2. Honor through:
Selection

9. Live through:
Integrity

3. Know through:
Prediction

8. Serve through:
Procedure

4. See through:
Promise

7. Love through:
Harmony

5. Hear through:
Kinship

6. Speak through:
Patience

TRUTH

LOVE   PEACE

CAUSE   EFFECT

Core:

North
Wisdom through:
Counseling

West
Future through:
Security

East
Inspiration through:
Persistence

FOCUS

EARTH   PATH

South
Lessons through:
Envisioning

Lynx
Decree of Logic

Lynx had a series of lessons that spelled out his Decree. The first lesson came as a surprise when Lynx went hunting. Lynx was stalking a prey he really couldn't see. Being hungry, he had no thought of competition. Mountain Lion was stalking from another direction. What a surprise when their eyes met, each was stalking the other. Lynx sped away as Mountain Lion lost him in the tangled bushes. Lynx remembered from that day to practice self-awareness in relation to tracking for prey.

Later, Lynx was foraging for food. His logic told him to be near water. This time Lynx was careless and was almost carried over a high waterfall. "I need to practice my sense of self-awareness," thought Lynx as he struggled out of the water.

One day while resting under an aromatic pine, the Tree spoke to Lynx.

Self-awareness can be learned,
Self-knowledge can be learned from trust.
Self-reliance can be earned,
Self-preservation is a must.

Sense awareness comes with sharing,
Inner trust provides the caring.
Lack of faith creates the heartsick,
Spiritual touch heals with logic.

Lynx listened as the Tree repeated the message again and again.

From that time on, Lynx visited the Wisdom Tree to reinforce the lessons. Every time he sleeps there, the same voice speaks to him of the Lynx Decree.

Da Naho!

Moose

Contribution -Judgment

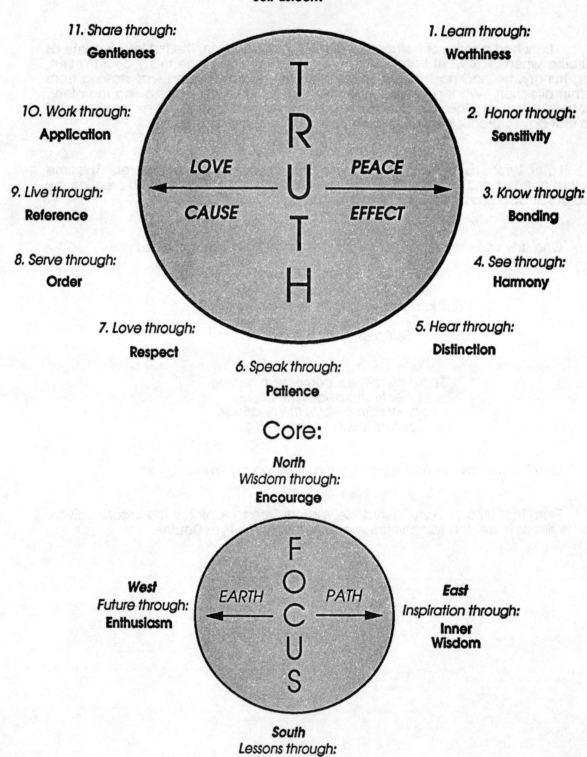

12. Thank through:
Self-Esteem

11. Share through:
Gentleness

1. Learn through:
Worthiness

10. Work through:
Application

2. Honor through:
Sensitivity

LOVE   *PEACE*

9. Live through:
Reference

CAUSE   *EFFECT*

3. Know through:
Bonding

8. Serve through:
Order

4. See through:
Harmony

7. Love through:
Respect

5. Hear through:
Distinction

6. Speak through:
Patience

T
R
U
T
H

Core:

North
Wisdom through:
Encourage

West
Future through:
Enthusiasm

EARTH   *PATH*

East
Inspiration through:
Inner Wisdom

F
O
C
U
S

South
Lessons through:
Experience

Moose
Decree of Judgment

Judgment lies in the intuitive self.
Self-esteem is faith, inspired through health.

Survival is instinct, its beauty is kinship. The Decree of Moose occurred where learning began. It was the time Creatures emerged from the water. Moose is akin to Deer, but larger.

There was a time in Moose memory that a stampede occurred. The thundering hooves leaped over a cliff, and this band was completely lost. But where they landed on top of each other, a miracle happened. Their spirits survived and rose to be heard.

When thoughts become blind and follows a leader
Look for the reason and be your own teacher.
Caring is sharing, the instinct of life
Judgment is wisdom, the inquest of strife.

It was then, Moose spirit descended into the physical world to create a Balance in Living. Each time the white Moose is seen the Decree is reinforced.

Da Naho!

Mountain Lion

Contribution -Leaderhip

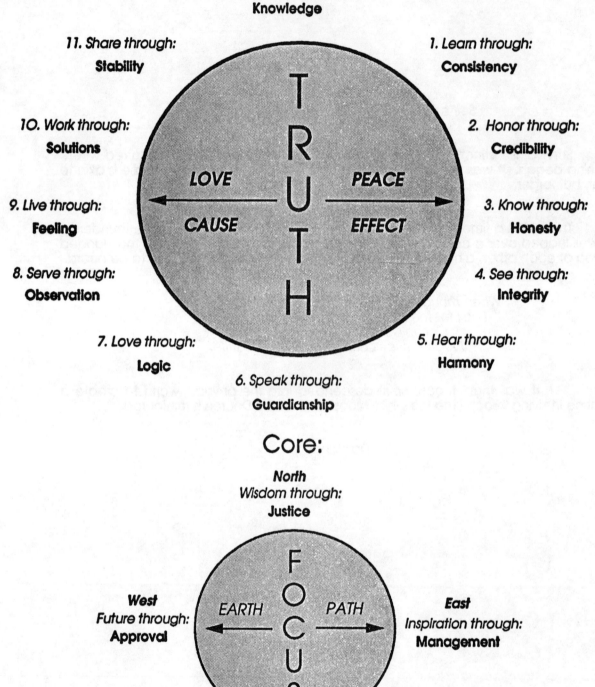

12. Thank through:
Knowledge

11. Share through:
Stability

1. Learn through:
Consistency

10. Work through:
Solutions

2. Honor through:
Credibility

9. Live through:
Feeling

3. Know through:
Honesty

8. Serve through:
Observation

4. See through:
Integrity

7. Love through:
Logic

5. Hear through:
Harmony

6. Speak through:
Guardianship

LOVE — **TRUTH** — *PEACE*
CAUSE — *EFFECT*

Core:

North
Wisdom through:
Justice

West
Future through:
Approval

East
Inspiration through:
Management

South
Lessons through:
Perception

EARTH — **FOCUS** — *PATH*

Mountain Lion
Decree of Leadership

The Mountain Lion enters where others fear to tread,
Where fears are washed away and trust is fed.
Mountain Lion moves into unseen space,
Enlightening the path to feel its embrace.

Mountain Lion works on his very own,
Planting the thought, for the future to hone.
Mountain Lion walks with Earth's nightly dream,
Where peace is the nugget, the leader's theme.

Mountain Lion sets a natural pace,
That all may walk in their Sacred Space.

There came a time when Mountain Lion needed leadership. His bigness got in his way. One time, Mountain Lion entered a cave where the Bats lived. The walls were resting places for the Bats. They had followed their Decree and made their sleeping place safe. When Mountain Lion brushed against the side of the cave, he injured the Bats. In an effort for the Bats to move to a safer place, they brushed against Mountain Lion who roared in his defense, and deafened the sensitive hearing system of the Bats. Frenzied in pain, the Bats flew in every direction, chasing Mountain Lion from the cave.

Learn about your gifts, to make you understand,
Life can be secure when living is at hand.
Bungling and roaring can lead to inner fear.
Open your eyes and heart, Peace is always near.

From that day on, Mountain Lion learned who he was,
He began to find the right reason for a pause.
Time passed slowly as lessons he learned
To prove this wisdom, his leadership was earned.

Da Nahol

Mouse

Contribution -Bravery

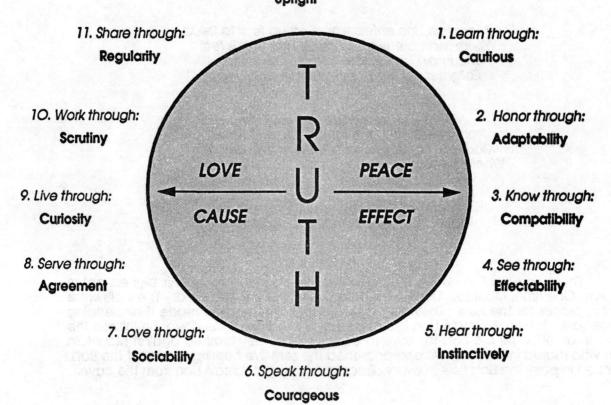

12. Thank through:
Upright

11. Share through:
Regularity

1. Learn through:
Cautious

10. Work through:
Scrutiny

2. Honor through:
Adaptability

LOVE | PEACE
CAUSE | EFFECT

TRUTH

9. Live through:
Curiosity

3. Know through:
Compatibility

8. Serve through:
Agreement

4. See through:
Effectability

7. Love through:
Sociability

5. Hear through:
Instinctively

6. Speak through:
Courageous

Core:

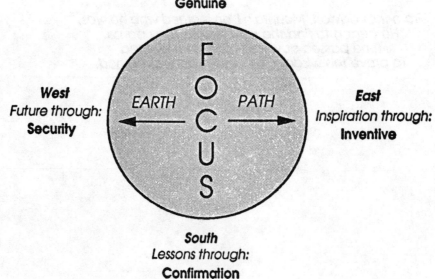

North
Wisdom through:
Genuine

West
Future through:
Security

EARTH | PATH

FOCUS

East
Inspiration through:
Inventive

South
Lessons through:
Confirmation

Mouse
Decree of Bravery

It happened at nighttime, when Mouse was free,
To visit strange places where he shouldn't be.
He ran into a Wolf den, a Wolf residency,
And found a hungry Wolf with a family.

She was quite busy feeding her new litter,
Her pups were very small but Mouse was bigger.
She sniffed at his nose and was about to bite,
Mouse squalled like her kin, this made things right.

Mouse nestled beside Wolf as a hungry pup,
He nursed with the pups and drank the milk up.
His body was filled and the fattest at best,
He grunted approval just like the rest.

Needless to say, he wasn't concerned,
This new comfort station he had earned.
But when the sleepers began to move,
They shoved him into a vacant groove.

Next thing he knew, he was in Wolf mouth,
He bit her tongue, squalling "I want out."
She gnashed her teeth, he thought he was a goner,
And coughed him up as he squalled "so long."

The following day he returned to the den,
And climbed on Wolf's nose and asked "be my friend?"
She looked into his unfaltering eyes,
And answered "yes" to his greatest surprise.

He learned to be courageous because of this,
Now Mouse can go any place and hit or miss.
Just set him up with a place that's tough,
And watch his system of using courageous stuff.

Da Nahol

Opossum

Contribution -Diversion

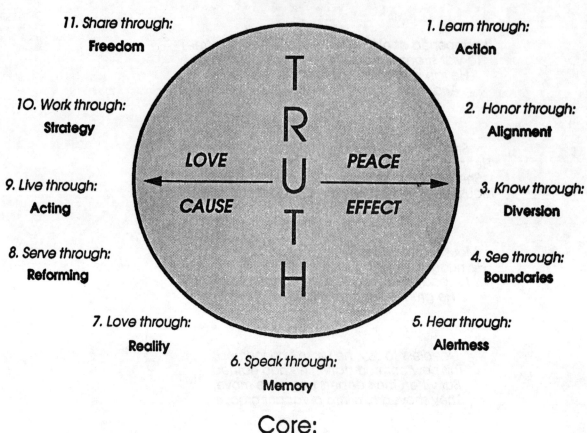

12. Thank through:
Protecting

11. Share through:
Freedom

1. Learn through:
Action

10. Work through:
Strategy

2. Honor through:
Alignment

LOVE   PEACE

TRUTH

CAUSE   EFFECT

9. Live through:
Acting

3. Know through:
Diversion

8. Serve through:
Reforming

4. See through:
Boundaries

7. Love through:
Reality

5. Hear through:
Alertness

6. Speak through:
Memory

Core:

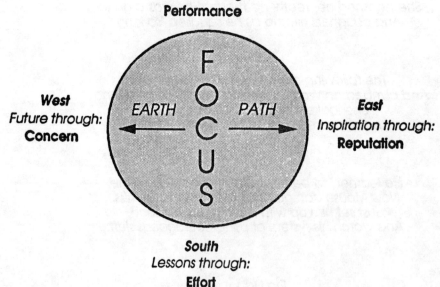

North
Wisdom through:
Performance

West
Future through:
Concern

EARTH   PATH

FOCUS

East
Inspiration through:
Reputation

South
Lessons through:
Effort

Opossum
Decree of Diversion

Many Moons ago, a Clan of Opossum were moving to a new location, due to overcrowding of their forest home.   A Council was held to make the move into a strange land.   At this Council, great quarreling was taking place and no decisions were being made.

Suddenly, Hinoh the Thunderer sounded his great voice and told the noisy Opossum to listen, for he had words of wisdom in the form of a Decree.

Move during the darkness as not to be seen,
Diversion is to support one's self-esteem.
Families stay whole when not too hasty,
Being a community secures their safety.
Should you be forced to move by day,
Play dead so that others stay away.

The Opossums were silenced by this great wisdom and learned this lesson in how to listen.

Stay in your environment each happy day,
And feel body-comfort in a natural way.

Da Naho!

Otter

Contribution -Enthusiasm

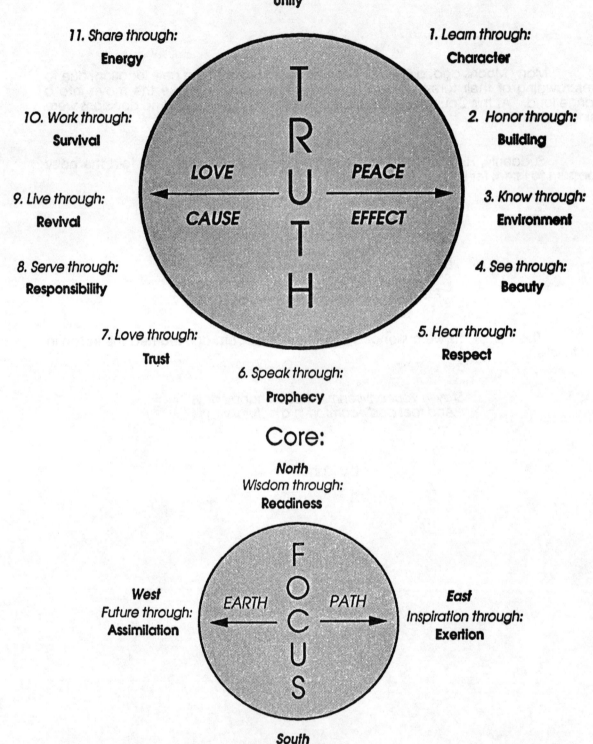

12. Thank through:
Unity

11. Share through:
Energy

1. Learn through:
Character

10. Work through:
Survival

2. Honor through:
Building

9. Live through:
Revival

3. Know through:
Environment

8. Serve through:
Responsibility

4. See through:
Beauty

7. Love through:
Trust

5. Hear through:
Respect

6. Speak through:
Prophecy

TRUTH

LOVE   *PEACE*
CAUSE   *EFFECT*

Core:

North
Wisdom through:
Readiness

West
Future through:
Assimilation

East
Inspiration through:
Exertion

South
Lessons through:
Principles

FOCUS

EARTH   *PATH*

Otter

Decree of Enthusiasm

Having fun is the Wisdom.
Learning awakens those who play.
When joining talents into one,
Enthusiasm has begun.

Long ago, Otter thought he had more enthusiasm than any other Creature. He boasted about this to his neighbors, Weasel and Mink. This boasting bothered Weasel and Mink and they told Otter to prove his statement.

"In order to have enthusiasm one needs wisdom. I am wisest of all," boasted Otter.

"You can't have wisdom unless you have skills" chided Weasel.

"I have both wisdom and skills," added Mink.

The arguing became louder and louder. Hinoh, the Thunder heard the commotion.

"Otter, prove your statement right now!" Hinoh roared.

Otter swam to the center of his pond where the youngers were playing.

"Gather around me," he ordered. "Our reputation is at stake. We have to prove to Weasel and Mink how we express our enthusiasm."

When Otter finished, the youngers began to slap their tails against the water and the sound filled the air.

"Stop!" ordered Otter. "I know how we can prove to everyone what great enthusiasm we have. Let's hit our tails against the water and sing songs at the same time. We'll do this by swimming in a circle.

Otter swam to the center of the pond while the youngers formed a circle around him. He held his tail high to start the rhythm. He flapped his tail first and the youngers followed by slapping their tails with the same time. This set up a rhythm of one - two; one - two that resounded throughout the woodlands. Creatures from everywhere listened and were united by the steady cadence of the rhythm. They recognized that the same rhythm came from the beating of their hearts. To honor Hinoh for asking the Otter to prove his statement, they sang:

Hinoh - Hinoh - weo heh, Hinoh
Gi we ooh - Gi we ooh

It is said that the Otter were the first to recognize the rhythmic heartbeat that flowed throughout the world.

Enthusiasm - Enthusiasm
Energizes fun.
Enthusiasm - Enthusiasm
Belongs to everyone.

Da Naho!

Owl

Contribution -Questioning

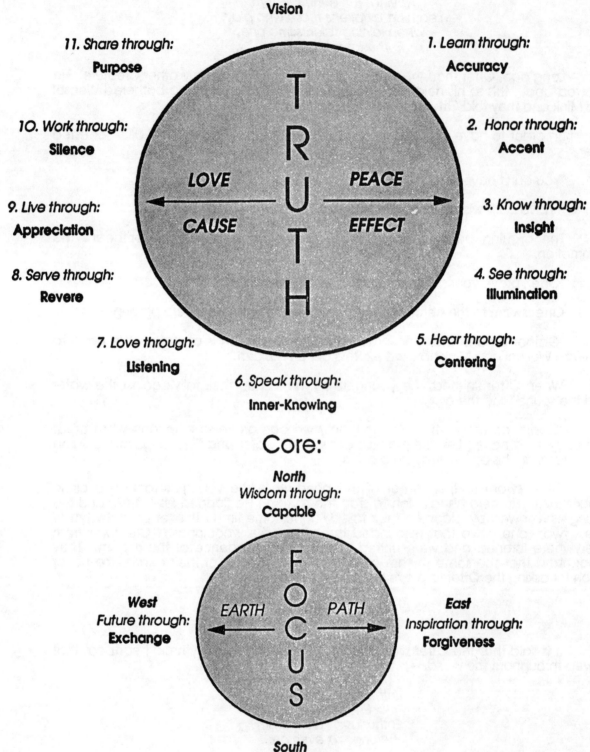

12. *Thank through:*
Vision

11. *Share through:*
Purpose

1. *Learn through:*
Accuracy

10. *Work through:*
Silence

2. *Honor through:*
Accent

LOVE   PEACE

9. *Live through:*
Appreciation

CAUSE   EFFECT

3. *Know through:*
Insight

8. *Serve through:*
Revere

4. *See through:*
Illumination

7. *Love through:*
Listening

5. *Hear through:*
Centering

6. *Speak through:*
Inner-Knowing

Core:

North
Wisdom through:
Capable

West
Future through:
Exchange

EARTH   PATH

East
Inspiration through:
Forgiveness

South
Lessons through:
Confidence

Owl
Decree of Questioning

Many Moons ago, all Creature Beings sounded alike. It was hard to understand who was talking or even what they had to say. One time Wolf and Owl were listening to the monotonous sound. Wolf commented, "What good is it to be able to speak when everyone sounds the same?"

"Speak for yourself Wolf. I'm satisfied," answered Owl.

Hinoh, the Thunder Chief, heard the strange conversation and decided to do something about it. Hinoh sang through the trees in his melodic voice.

Wolf said, "Listen to the voice."

"It does have a certain personality," responded Owl.

"How would you like to sound like that?" thundered Hinoh from above.

"Of course I would," promptly answered Owl.

"Hold your mouth open and I will use my lightening rod to charge your throat. The sound you make will be different from all the other Creature Beings," explained Hinoh.

"Will it hurt?" asked Owl.

"Try it, and like it!" howled Hinoh.

"The lightening stick opened Owl's throat and he began saying "who!"

Wolf was so amazed he asked Hinoh for the same treatment. When the other Creatures heard Owl and Wolf's new voices, Hinoh was busy unlocking the voices of all the Creatures.

This was the beginning of Owl and Wolf's Voice Wisdom. To this day, everyone is intrigued by Owl and Wolf's calls.

Da Naho!

Porcupine

Contribution -Faith

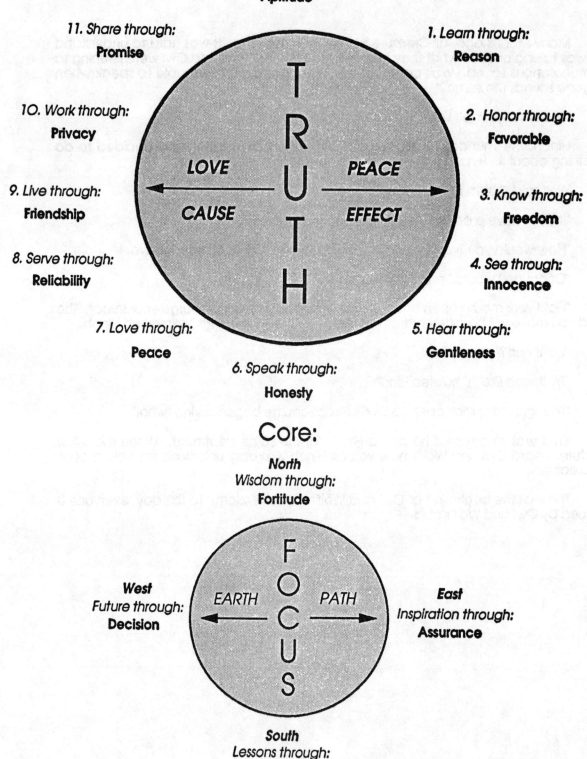

12. Thank through:
Aptitude

11. Share through:
Promise

1. Learn through:
Reason

10. Work through:
Privacy

2. Honor through:
Favorable

LOVE   *PEACE*

CAUSE   *EFFECT*

9. Live through:
Friendship

3. Know through:
Freedom

8. Serve through:
Reliability

4. See through:
Innocence

7. Love through:
Peace

5. Hear through:
Gentleness

6. Speak through:
Honesty

Core:

North
Wisdom through:
Fortitude

West
Future through:
Decision

EARTH   *PATH*

East
Inspiration through:
Assurance

South
Lessons through:
Selection

Porcupine
Decree of Faith

Faith becomes a friendly gift,
Non-aggression shapes the way.
Self- appraisal frames the shift,
While self-esteem honors the day.

Porcupine liked to visit friends, who lived in faraway places. These friends enjoyed Porcupine's innocence because he was pure of heart. It happened that Porcupine was a Bird who liked to sit in trees. But sitting in trees didn't satisfy his hunger, and he was forced to visit Motherearth for food. As time passed, Porcupine came to a point in his life when he needed to make a decision. He would either continue being a Bird, or take on qualities of a Four-Legged.

"You mean I have a choice?" he asked, for the voice within had spoken.

"I'll have to put my mind at rest, in this dynamic notion." Putting his mind to rest was hard, as his mind played with his wits.

"How would my beak become a nose, and two legs change to four?" asked Porcupine.

"You need not think about this change, because it is done in a roar!" Spoke Hinoh the Thunder Chief.

Porcupine liked to be close to Earth and began to like the idea. The time drew near for the changeover. All the Forest Creatures came to see the transformation.

Within a flash Porcupine sprouted two more legs, and a white, handsome snout. But something had happened, he still had feathers on his back, which made him a curious sight!

"Don't worry about that," said Hinoh. "The feathers will wear off." And sure enough they did. To this day they are quills, and they serve as a reminder of what Porcupine used to be.

We look like we want to be,
Our thoughts express the vision.
We feel just what we want to feel,
And cast the final decision.

Da Naho!

Rabbit

Contribution -Strategy

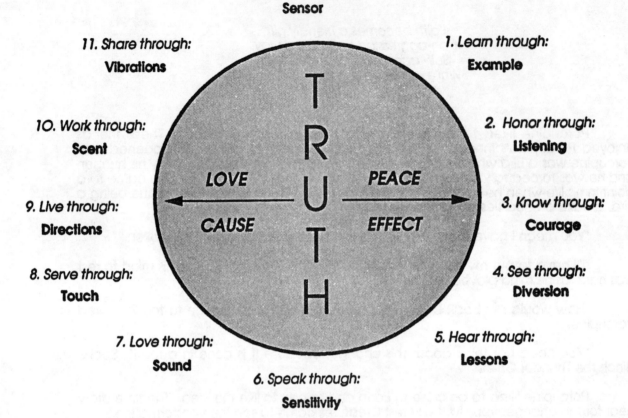

12. *Thank through:*
Sensor

11. *Share through:*
Vibrations

1. *Learn through:*
Example

10. *Work through:*
Scent

2. *Honor through:*
Listening

9. *Live through:*
Directions

3. *Know through:*
Courage

8. *Serve through:*
Touch

4. *See through:*
Diversion

7. *Love through:*
Sound

5. *Hear through:*
Lessons

6. *Speak through:*
Sensitivity

LOVE   PEACE
CAUSE   EFFECT

T R U T H

Core:

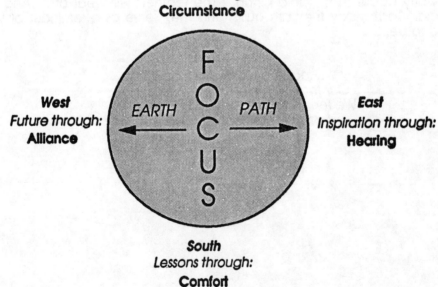

North
Wisdom through:
Circumstance

West
Future through:
Alliance

East
Inspiration through:
Hearing

South
Lessons through:
Comfort

EARTH   PATH

F O C U S

Rabbit
Decree of Strategy

A Rabbit Decree had been received when Grandfather Rabbit was chased by a tree. Now this might seem rather strange but according to Grandfather Rabbit it occurred to him.

It happened that Grandfather Rabbit couldn't sleep so he crept out of his sleeping place to take a night walk. When Grandmother Moon saw him she smiled, creating tree shadows in the forest. We must remember that shadows are friendly creatures.

When the wind blew that night, the tree shadows chased Grandfather Rabbit. Frightened, he stumbled over a sleeping tree stump and bumped his head as he fell. The fall made him dizzy.

"Trees can't run," he thought. After shaking off his fear, he returned to the tree. The second time the wind blew and Grandfather Rabbit was again chased by the tree shadows. This time he jumped clear of the sleeping stump and rammed into a tree. He shook his fear off and returned to the tree.

"Why are you chasing me?" he asked the tree. Tree spoke.

To honor a Rabbit Decree
That Gifts your kind with strategy
From this time on make Rabbit tracks
And stop your looking for Rabbit snacks.

Rabbit didn't know what Tree meant. Later on Grandfather Rabbit was eating when he felt that someone was looking at him. He turned around and saw Wolf. When Wolf was about to eat him, he zigzagged his escape and safely reached his burrow. Wolf was digging at Rabbit's door. "Wolf, I outwitted you. I'm safe and full and you're still hungry." "I can wait, I have strategy," answered Wolf. "My strategy is better than yours," boasted Rabbit. "We'll see," responded the Wolf.

Now what Rabbit didn't know was that there were two Wolves. When Rabbit jumped from the other end of his burrow, the second Wolf gave chase. Rabbit zigzagged toward the end of his burrow and saw the second Wolf. "Ahah!" said second Wolf. "Now who has the better strategy?" "I have," Rabbit boldly answered and immediately howled like the Wolves. "I am one of your kind," he said standing between the two Wolves.

The first Wolf said, "We don't eat our kind." "There are two of you. It's two against one." The second Wolf responded, "You must be a Wolf. We like things even." "That's right," said Rabbit as he turned to enter his burrow. Wolf said, "That was a strange looking Wolf...I have just proved that I'm the master strategist."

From the day, Wolf has always chased Rabbits to practice Wolf strategy.

Da Nahol

Raccoon

Contribution -Protection

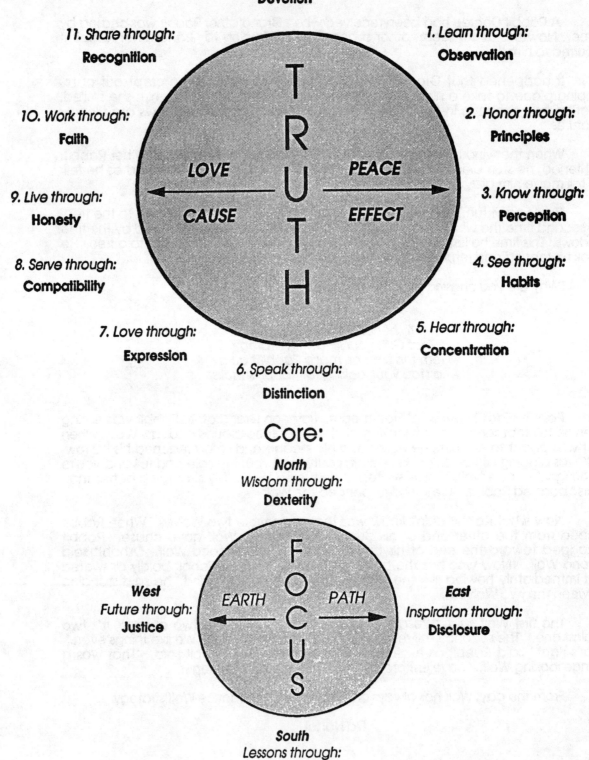

12. Thank through:
Devotion

11. Share through:
Recognition

1. Learn through:
Observation

10. Work through:
Faith

2. Honor through:
Principles

9. Live through:
Honesty

3. Know through:
Perception

8. Serve through:
Compatibility

4. See through:
Habits

7. Love through:
Expression

5. Hear through:
Concentration

6. Speak through:
Distinction

TRUTH

LOVE — *PEACE*

CAUSE — *EFFECT*

Core:

North
Wisdom through:
Dexterity

West
Future through:
Justice

East
Inspiration through:
Disclosure

FOCUS

EARTH — *PATH*

South
Lessons through:
Integrity

Raccoon
Decree of Protection

The Raccoon family of Protection,
Revealed their living through Group Expression.
Raccoons are thriving, Peaceful and mature,
Their place in all Nature is Pure and Secure.

A time came when Raccoon was tested for sharing his place in society. Lodging places and food were becoming scarce. It was then that Raccoon changed his lifestyle from being a day species to a night species. This made lodging places more easily shared and distributed.

Raccoon had special front feet that looked like hands. Whenever his family came to a hazardous place, Raccoon raised his hands to make others stop while his family proceeded in safety.

One day a man was driving down a hill and saw Raccoon standing in the middle of the road. The man stopped his car while another man coming from the opposite direction did the same. Both drivers watched the Raccoon family cross the road. When the Raccoon family safely reached the other side of the road, Raccoon followed. One of the men stated: "Now I know why so many Raccoons are killed on the road. They are protecting their families."

Da Nahol

Raven

Contribution -Change

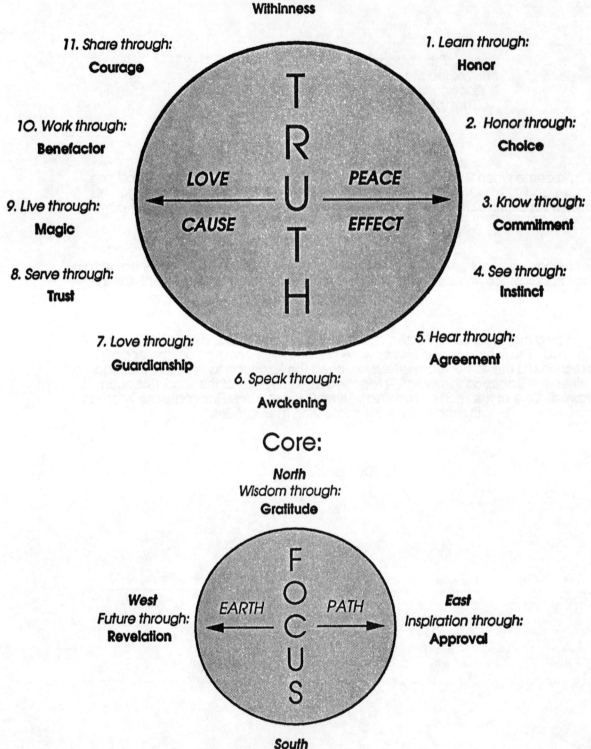

12. *Thank through:*
Withinness

11. *Share through:*
Courage

1. *Learn through:*
Honor

10. *Work through:*
Benefactor

2. *Honor through:*
Choice

LOVE   PEACE

9. *Live through:*
Magic

CAUSE   EFFECT

3. *Know through:*
Commitment

TRUTH

4. *See through:*
Instinct

8. *Serve through:*
Trust

5. *Hear through:*
Agreement

7. *Love through:*
Guardianship

6. *Speak through:*
Awakening

Core:

North
Wisdom through:
Gratitude

FOCUS

West
Future through:
Revelation

EARTH   PATH

East
Inspiration through:
Approval

South
Lessons through:
Obedience

Raven
Decree of Change

Raven, Raven soaring high,
A messenger of the ebony sky.
The listener, thinker, silence bound,
The pathfinder, seeker, sender of sound.

Raven melts into the environment with freedom of flight, with penetrating eyes and magical sight. Raven received his Decree of change, at a time when the Sky World was absent of Grandmother Moon and Stars. A voice was heard from deep within ...

Raven, Raven who sees in the night,
Senses the trials of hunger and blight.
Raven warns of incoming changes,
And what to do for change that ages.
Directing change a focused door,
Reveals the Truth for evermore.

Since that time the Raven has been a Messenger of Change. The black, incandescent feathers are "Seeking the Light of Truth". Raven the benefactor exemplifies patience.

Patience lives in Raven's heart,
Where it grows shall not depart.
Love, Truth and Peace from the Sacred Band,
It's the place where growth began.

When one walks into life's darkness, the Raven gives thought of courage and strength, through a lovely heart to build inner Peace where the foundation of Truth supports one's life span.

Da Naho!

Sheep

Contribution -Companionship

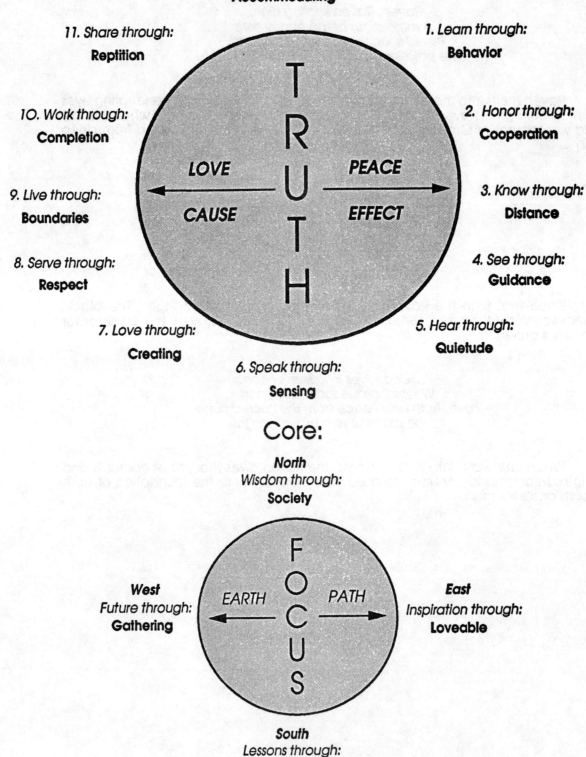

12. Thank through:
Accommodating

11. Share through:
Reptition

1. Learn through:
Behavior

10. Work through:
Completion

2. Honor through:
Cooperation

LOVE   PEACE

TRUTH

CAUSE   EFFECT

9. Live through:
Boundaries

3. Know through:
Distance

8. Serve through:
Respect

4. See through:
Guidance

7. Love through:
Creating

5. Hear through:
Quietude

6. Speak through:
Sensing

Core:

North
Wisdom through:
Society

FOCUS

West
Future through:
Gathering

EARTH   PATH

East
Inspiration through:
Loveable

South
Lessons through:
Friendship

Sheep
Decree of Companionship

Hinoh watched Sheep in all kinds of weather moving from place to place seemingly, with no purpose in living. "It's time for a Decree," Hinoh spoke loud and clear.

A leader must emerge from your kind,
And with virtue within his/her mind.
Strong hearted, loving and sure-footed,
Patient, non-aggressive and earth rooted.

The Two-Leggeds will be your overseer,
You will live among them where life is freer.
Wool for clothing your bodies will provide,
Mutton, as a food, you'll be known worldwide.

Sheep shall be herded into fields and dales,
Grazing and resting in fertile swales.
You will be shepherded into a flock,
Sheep shall be decreed as the first livestock.

The Sheep listened to the distinctive voice,
Immediately, they knew they had no choice.
They wanted to live in a docile way,
Sheep had received this Decree as man's prey.

From that time, Sheep have honored their mission,
By carrying on their Sacred vision.
Life of abundance has quickened them now,
As they pursued their companionship vow."

Hinoh has spoken.

Da Naho!

Skunk

Contribution -Gentleness

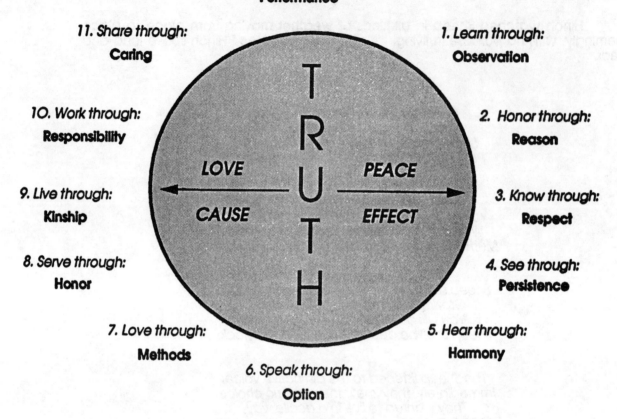

12. Thank through:
Performance

11. Share through:
Caring

1. Learn through:
Observation

10. Work through:
Responsibility

2. Honor through:
Reason

LOVE **TRUTH** *PEACE*

CAUSE *EFFECT*

9. Live through:
Kinship

3. Know through:
Respect

8. Serve through:
Honor

4. See through:
Persistence

7. Love through:
Methods

5. Hear through:
Harmony

6. Speak through:
Option

Core:

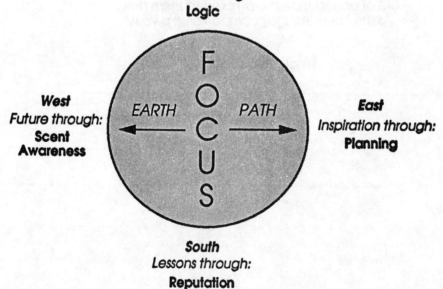

North
Wisdom through:
Logic

West
Future through:
Scent
Awareness

EARTH **FOCUS** *PATH*

East
Inspiration through:
Planning

South
Lessons through:
Reputation

Skunk

Decree of Gentleness

There was a special feeling that permeated the Woodlands when Skunk joined the Creature Beings. The small black-and-white streaked Creatures walked on Mother Earth as if they were tracking Sacred Ground. Wherever they went this peaceful attitude left its mark. Then one day an unhealthy feeling pressed upon the Earth Creatures. They were choking and feeling dread.

"What's happening?" called the living Creatures. "What's causing this choking plague?"

A voice spoke. "The Skunks have received their Wisdom, now Council to receive their Decree."

> Gentleness must have protection, that non other can see,
> A sudden stench of impurities defile the pure and free.
> Skunk sends its aroma to overcome the smell,
> Clarify the air so that other breeds can dwell.

The putrification, it has been said, that attacked the air was nullified from Skunk aroma. To this day Skunks protect themselves by excreting a powerful odor. Skunk has maintained a reputation of respect.

Da Naho!

Snake

Contribution -Transformation

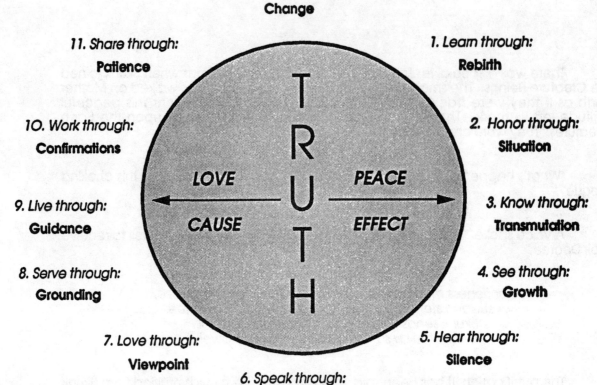

12. Thank through:
Change

11. Share through:
Patience

1. Learn through:
Rebirth

10. Work through:
Confirmations

2. Honor through:
Situation

LOVE · PEACE
CAUSE · EFFECT
TRUTH

9. Live through:
Guidance

3. Know through:
Transmutation

8. Serve through:
Grounding

4. See through:
Growth

7. Love through:
Viewpoint

5. Hear through:
Silence

6. Speak through:
Principles

Core:

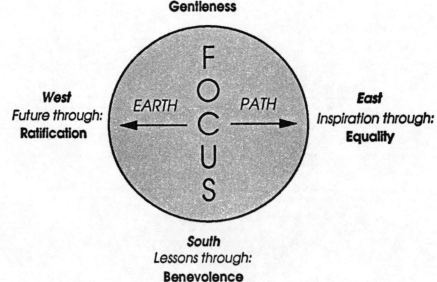

North
Wisdom through:
Gentleness

West
Future through:
Ratification

EARTH · PATH
FOCUS

East
Inspiration through:
Equality

South
Lessons through:
Benevolence

Snake
Decree of Transformation

Change is grounded equally
It begins with all forms of life.
Wisdom heals the hurt within
Love sends away all strife.

Snake is coiled at the Vibral Core,
The center of all feeling presence.
Snake transmuted within the within
With spiritual convalescence.

Snake appeared to rock with a question to be heard: "When did we enter and when did we learn the stone is the Vibral Core of the environmental dimension?"

The core is the root to which we are all aligned,
The expenditors are sounds encoded with time.

We must be grounded to exact change in spirit,
It must occur simultaneously to hear it.
The Male/Female centering creates perfect transmutation,
Snake is the example of the magic gift of transformation.

Once Snake had a different coat that was tied to himself. Time and time again he tore at his coat as it confined his expanding whim from within. One day he slipped into a mire that coated his outer skin. Rains came from the Outer World and released his tainted whim.

The first time he looked at himself he loved himself from within. And to this day, Snake looks for the time he can release his outer skin.

Da Naho!

Snipe

Contribution -Discipline

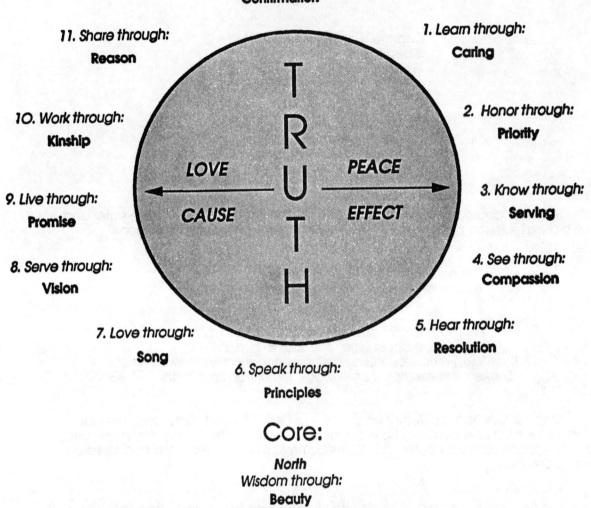

12. Thank through:
Confirmation

11. Share through:
Reason

1. Learn through:
Caring

10. Work through:
Kinship

2. Honor through:
Priority

LOVE   *PEACE*

T R U T H

CAUSE   *EFFECT*

9. Live through:
Promise

3. Know through:
Serving

8. Serve through:
Vision

4. See through:
Compassion

7. Love through:
Song

5. Hear through:
Resolution

6. Speak through:
Principles

Core:

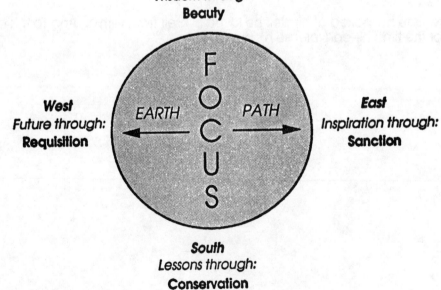

North
Wisdom through:
Beauty

F O C U S

EARTH   *PATH*

West
Future through:
Requisition

East
Inspiration through:
Sanction

South
Lessons through:
Conservation

Snipe
Degree of Discipline

All the Wingeds had received a message of the Great Council. The Sky World was almost darkened when the Wingeds gathered to hear the Decree. The Snipe had practiced all their gifts, for they had heard the chiefs of all the Feathered People would be chosen. The Snipes were proud of their plumes, that distinguished them among other wingeds.

We have beauty for all to see,
It's the image that sets us free.
We are gifted with ideal flight,
That secures our noble sight.

These thoughts of pride had made the other Feather Clans shun the Snipe. Yet they were certain no other Feather People could match their beauty.

Eagle was the speaker ...

Feathered Clans we hold Council here,
And sing our songs of worldly cheer.
Our song shall reach every land,
Bonding Peace through the Feathered Clan.

When the Snipes stood in the Council Ring, their feathered plumes were not seen. To remedy this condition the Snipes painfully pulled out each other's tail plumes, and pushed the quills between the feathers on their heads. Thus their heads displayed the plumes where they could be better seen. Consequently, their balance was effected, and when they approached the center of the Council, their walk created laughter. As they walked their heads bobbed down and their tails stuck up. The Four Winds were there and when they laughed, the feathers flew from the Snipes heads, causing embarrassment and the Snipes to run from view.

The lesson learned from this experience is that we must honor how we look, and not change our natural image.

We enter into this birth walk, to touch the Earth,
Changing the image distorts our worth.
Life moves worthwhile in every way,
Growth serves Lifestyles on every day.

Eagle has spoken.

Da Naho!

Spider

Contribution -Networker

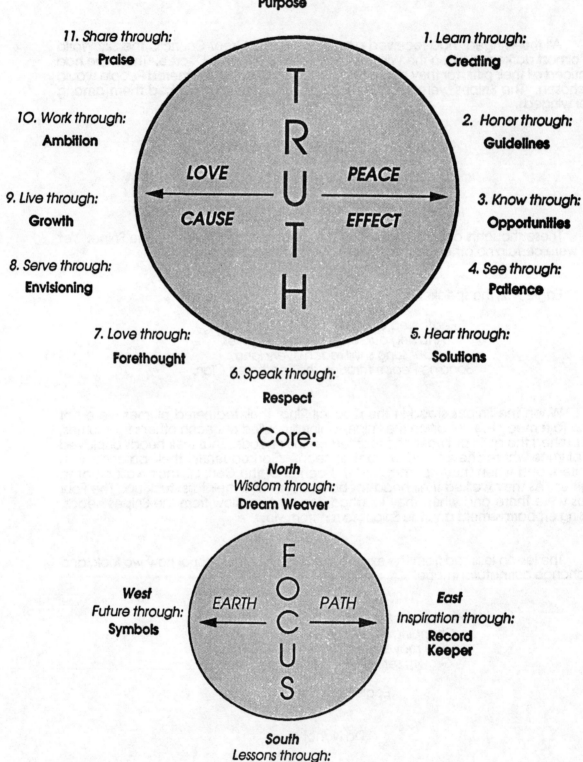

12. Thank through:
Purpose

11. Share through:
Praise

1. Learn through:
Creating

10. Work through:
Ambition

2. Honor through:
Guidelines

9. Live through:
Growth

3. Know through:
Opportunities

8. Serve through:
Envisioning

4. See through:
Patience

7. Love through:
Forethought

5. Hear through:
Solutions

6. Speak through:
Respect

LOVE   PEACE

CAUSE   EFFECT

TRUTH

Core:

North
Wisdom through:
Dream Weaver

West
Future through:
Symbols

East
Inspiration through:
Record Keeper

EARTH   PATH

FOCUS

South
Lessons through:
Weaving

Spider
Decree of the Networker

Spider weave my web of patience,
Spinning all inner radiance.
Spider keep promises of youth,
Reeling in the centering of Truth.

In the beginning, Spider left a thread-like substance wherever he had been. It was very good because Spider never became lost. But Spider didn't know what to do with the continuously unreeling thread attached to her body.

It happened that a great storm visited Natureland where all the creatures lived. Strong Winds spun Spider in a series of circles, round and round Spider twirled until she was dizzy. After the storm had quieted down, Spider looked at where she was. To her surprise she hung in the center of a web. Suddenly, the strong winds returned and blew into Spider's web. But it withheld the breath of the Winds which began to speak:

Spider, Spider spin your web for all others to see.
Spider, Spider spin a web to protect your family.
The time has come to receive your gift as a Decree.
Create your web as a working tool this wheel of life shall be.

The Winds have spoken.

Day after day, Spider practiced spinning the threads in symbols for others to see. Creature beings watched to see what Spider was doing. At long last she finished her web and sat in the middle.

Wind came and Spider web had withstood the strong breath. "You have reached your Decree of networking properly. This pattern shall be used for basket making to carry food for eternity."

The Wind Maker has spoken.

To this day, the web of Spider has become the foundation and pattern for making baskets.

Da Naho!

Squirrel
Contribution -The Gatherer

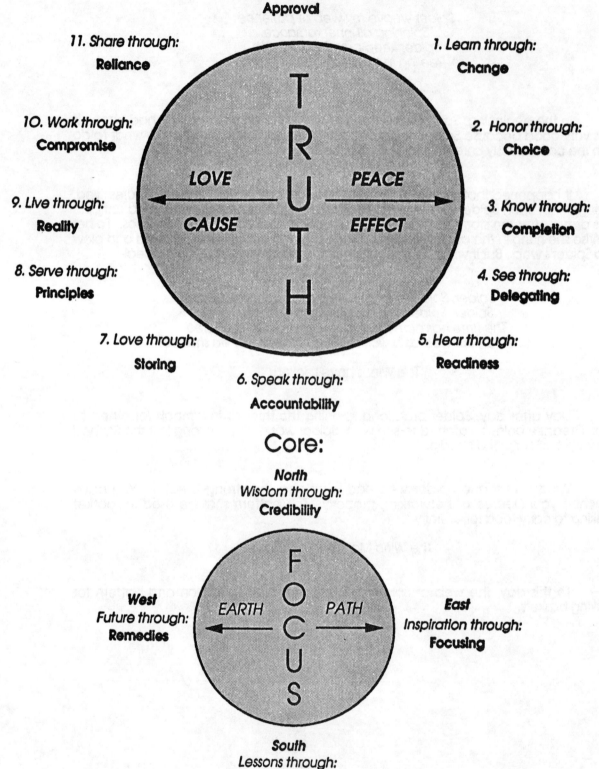

12. Thank through:
Approval

11. Share through:
Reliance

1. Learn through:
Change

10. Work through:
Compromise

2. Honor through:
Choice

LOVE   *PEACE*

T R U T H

CAUSE   *EFFECT*

9. Live through:
Reality

3. Know through:
Completion

8. Serve through:
Principles

4. See through:
Delegating

7. Love through:
Storing

5. Hear through:
Readiness

6. Speak through:
Accountability

Core:

North
Wisdom through:
Credibility

West
Future through:
Remedies

EARTH   *PATH*

F O C U S

East
Inspiration through:
Focusing

South
Lessons through:
Honor

Squirrel
Decree of the Gatherer

Squirrel gathered medicine beyond his smelling
He stored it in place without his telling.
Wherever Squirrel went he picked a new dwelling
And always seemed wise without his head swelling.

Squirrel was a Gatherer from the beginning. He was a hard worker and storing food was his major job. He always made way for the future life.

Squirrel was one of the first Creature Beings to receive a Decree. In the distant past when Creature Beings were being connected to the Earth, Squirrel was not too wise. He liked certain nuts and seeds. He ate them each and thought nothing about making plans for storage. The Squirrels were getting fatter and fatter. Soon, Wintertime came. Squirrel had not thought he'd be hungry when the cold time came. As a result, Squirrel experienced a hungry season.

Squirrels called a Council to assess their situation. During this Council, the Tree People were heard saying, "Tree People are prepared to announce a Decree."

Decaying trees may be used for storage of food. The Earth around the roots can support the food and increase the future as the seeds germinate. Roots and seeds go hand in hand. It's the future we serve to perpetuate each Clan.

Squirrel, you've been chosen to store nuts and seeds,
Your storing is endless and an example to see.
Make every decaying tree a storage place,
That trees are useful to embrace each living race.

The Tree People have spoken.

From that day on, every Squirrel works as a seeker of food and a Gatherer. Their storage efforts provides food for countless Creatures. And, the forgotten stored foods become plants so there is no loss.

Da Naho!

Swan

Contribution -Grace

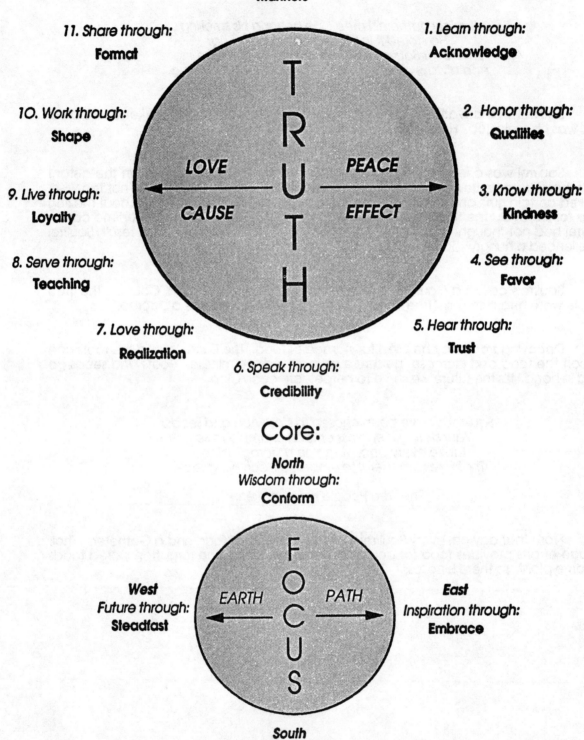

12. Thank through:
Manners

11. Share through:
Format

1. Learn through:
Acknowledge

10. Work through:
Shape

2. Honor through:
Qualities

LOVE   **PEACE**

9. Live through:
Loyalty

3. Know through:
Kindness

CAUSE   **EFFECT**

8. Serve through:
Teaching

4. See through:
Favor

7. Love through:
Realization

5. Hear through:
Trust

6. Speak through:
Credibility

Core:

North
Wisdom through:
Conform

West
Future through:
Steadfast

EARTH   **PATH**

East
Inspiration through:
Embrace

South
Lessons through:
Endurance

Swan
Decree of Grace

Swan was a big and ungainly Bird. Swan flew with the other Feathered Clans. He was the most clumsy of them all. Swan was quite unhappy because he wanted to belong with the rest, but he participated beyond his given capabilities.

Swan was a large, lanky Bird who looked clumsy when he flew into the Sky World. Other birds stayed away from Swan when they flew into the trees. However, while floating on the water, Swan moved about with very little effort. Swan could glide along and scarcely a ripple showed where he had been.

One day, as a Bluebird flew over the pond he became tired and landed on Swan's back. Swan looked at the Bluebird and remarked, "What beautiful blue feathers you have." Bluebird told Swan he was grateful for the gift of blue feathers bestowed upon him and then said to Swan, "What a wonderful gift you have to glide on the quiet pond with such grace."

Swan thought about what Bluebird had said and became happy as he realized that everyone has a particular gift of grace. We must learn to see ourselves as we are and not envy others.

Swan was happy for his grace,
And had a gift to embrace.
Gliding upon a glassy pond,
Made a union that's quite profound.

Da Naho!

Turkey

Contribution -Image

12. Thank through:
Agreement

11. Share through:
Promise

1. Learn through:
Curiosity

10. Work through:
Comfort

2. Honor through:
Endurance

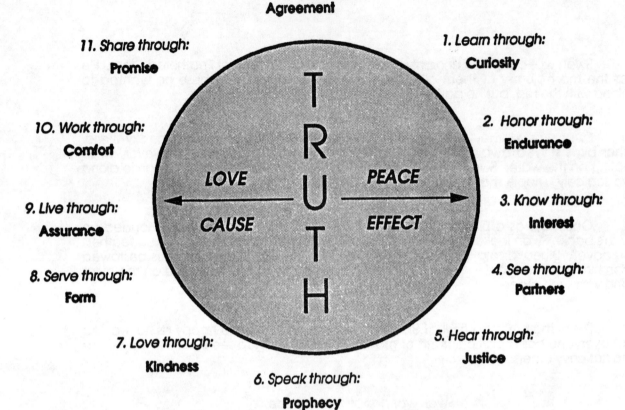

LOVE · PEACE
TRUTH
CAUSE · EFFECT

9. Live through:
Assurance

3. Know through:
Interest

8. Serve through:
Form

4. See through:
Partners

7. Love through:
Kindness

5. Hear through:
Justice

6. Speak through:
Prophecy

Core:

North
Wisdom through:
Upliftment

West
Future through:
Majestic

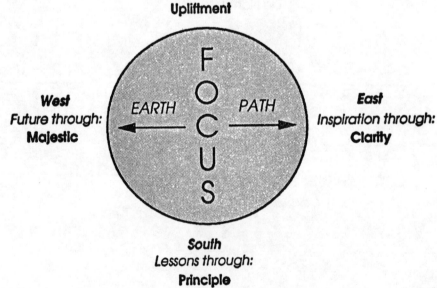

EARTH · PATH
FOCUS

East
Inspiration through:
Clarity

South
Lessons through:
Principle

Turkey
Decree of Image

The Turkey became a splendid fellow following this Decree:

Turkey, Turkey walking tall,
With your feathers of Peace.
Turkey, Turkey sing your call,
Inviting the spirits to dance with all.

Turkey became the Ground Eagle at the Council of the Wingeds. At that Council all the Wingeds flew. It was time for Turkey to fly. The big, heavy Turkey could not get himself off the ground. When he walked to the center of the Circle he said, "There's the Eagle up in Sky World. There needs to be one on Earth World." The Winged's Council agreed. To this day Turkey is honored as the Ground Eagle.

Turkey has given us many ceremonies of Honor. Turkey Feathers are used for regalia and as the Messengers of Peace. Turkey feathers bring Joy and Humor into a Council.

There were two gobbler Turkeys having a conversation in the Chicken yard. The first Turkey was boasting that he could attract any Chicken into his pen. The other Turkey was interested in how this big fellow could be attractive to Chickens. However, there were conditions. The second Gobbler could not see what the first was doing. After all, the second big Turkey was very interested in the first's boasting. Now, Chickens are very curious. The old Turkey knew this. He stepped into the corner of the chicken pen and began vigorously scratching the Earth and making sounds of appreciation. One chicken after another entered his pen to see what he was doing and when the second Turkey returned, he too entered the pens. The old Tom had proven his point and silently moved away with glee.

If we observed our Feathered friends, we'd learn much about our own reactions for our Feathered Friends have similar activities.

Da Nahol

Turtle

Contribution -Moral Code

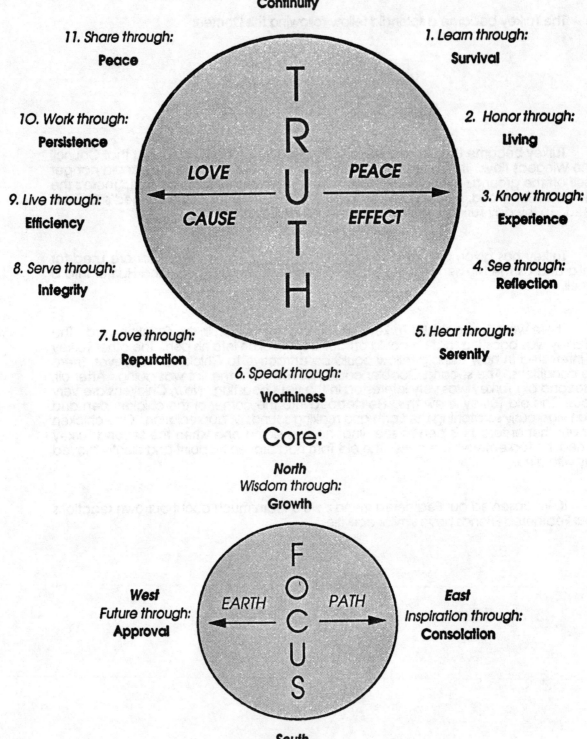

12. Thank through:
Continuity

11. Share through:
Peace

1. Learn through:
Survival

10. Work through:
Persistence

2. Honor through:
Living

LOVE T *PEACE*
R
U
CAUSE T *EFFECT*
H

9. Live through:
Efficiency

3. Know through:
Experience

8. Serve through:
Integrity

4. See through:
Reflection

7. Love through:
Reputation

5. Hear through:
Serenity

6. Speak through:
Worthiness

Core:

North
Wisdom through:
Growth

West
Future through:
Approval

F
O
EARTH C *PATH*
U
S

East
Inspiration through:
Consolation

South
Lessons through:
Renewal

Turtle
Decree of a Moral Code

Turtle, Turtle the slowest of them all,
Moves on his stomach so he cannot fall.
The Wisdom of the ages flows through his mind,
To teach a Moral Code one at a time.

Survival of the fittest is his creed,
His patience seeks to satisfy a need.
Turtle contribution is a Moral Code,
Setting into practice a Trusting Mode.

When Turtle first left the Water World to live upon the land, he found that it was quite cold and even wondered if he should have stayed in the water.

Grandfather Sun saw the dilemma that faced the Turtle and spoke to him.

"I'm the one who lights your world and warms it to make it feel comfortable. When you as a Turtle emerged from the Water World your body was soft and pliable. This body has no protection from Creatures who live out of water. I can help you to move on the Earth with safety as well as return you to the Water World. But there is something that you must promise me before I can perform this change. "What is it, what is it?" responded Turtle, excitedly.

There is a place called Waterland,
It lies at the center of Earth.
Turtle Island can be its name,
It's round and flat and with habitat.
It's up to you to discover its worth,
By making it a natural, livable berth.
Sun slipped behind the cloud,
Feeling love and mighty proud.

Turtle floated upon the water while Grandfather Sun hung in the Sky World. The softness of the Turtle's back began to bake by the warmth of Grandfather Sun. Soon his back was thoroughly baked yet the soft underside remained the same. Presently, Turtle felt his stomach hardening as he moved across the Earth.

"What is happening to me?" he thought.

You have accepted a Moral Code,
That sets a Truth within your abode.
As Peace Turtle, natural birth,
You're the beginning of Life on this Earth.

The Great Mystery has spoken.

Da Nahol

Weasel

Contribution -Adjustment

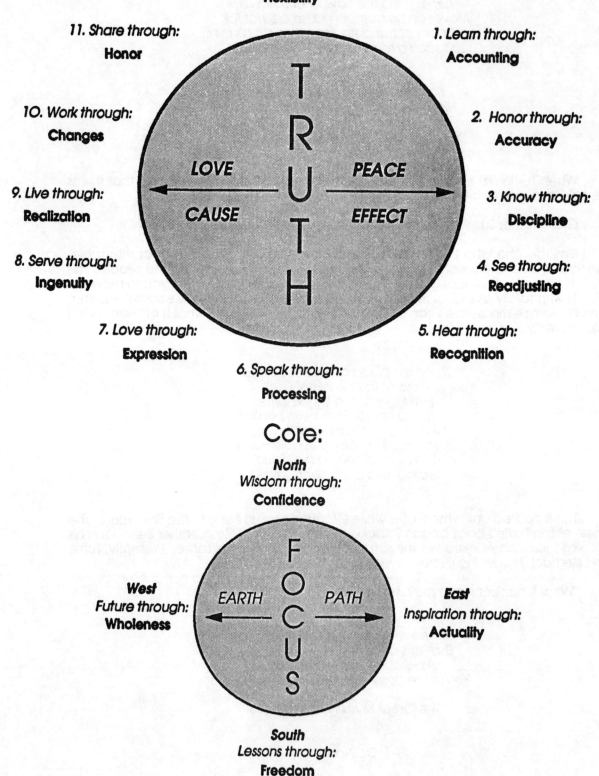

12. Thank through:
Flexibility

11. Share through:
Honor

1. Learn through:
Accounting

10. Work through:
Changes

2. Honor through:
Accuracy

LOVE   **TRUTH**   *PEACE*

CAUSE   *EFFECT*

9. Live through:
Realization

3. Know through:
Discipline

8. Serve through:
Ingenuity

4. See through:
Readjusting

7. Love through:
Expression

5. Hear through:
Recognition

6. Speak through:
Processing

Core:

North
Wisdom through:
Confidence

West
Future through:
Wholeness

EARTH   **FOCUS**   *PATH*

East
Inspiration through:
Actuality

South
Lessons through:
Freedom

Weasel
Decree of Adjustment

In times long forgotten, when animals were finding places to live, a Band of Weasels entered the Woodlands. They were living happily with their cousins the Skunks, to form a loving, gentle, trusting colony.

Life was peaceful until the cold time visited Motherearth. Weasel was food for larger critters, because they were playful and easily found. Soon they would learn a lesson through a Decree.

The Weasel families were fast disappearing, from lack of protection. Four Weasels in fear of being eaten, entered a dark cave, where they thought no one would see them. A Snake was coiled inside and asked. "What are you doing here?" Just then a Skunk crept into the cave, and released his protection sac. The stench was so horrifying, the Weasels fled from the cave into the snow. The Snow Chief had been watching and said ...

Weasel, Weasel sacred and small,
your Decree is 'one for all'.
When the snow has covered the ground,
Change your color and not be found.

Weasel had received his adjusting Decree, change is in the use of ingenuity.

From that time Weasels can change their fur to live within their surroundings. This adjustment has tapped into their Ingenuity. The White Weasel is called the Ermine.

Da Naho!

Whale

Contribution -Historian

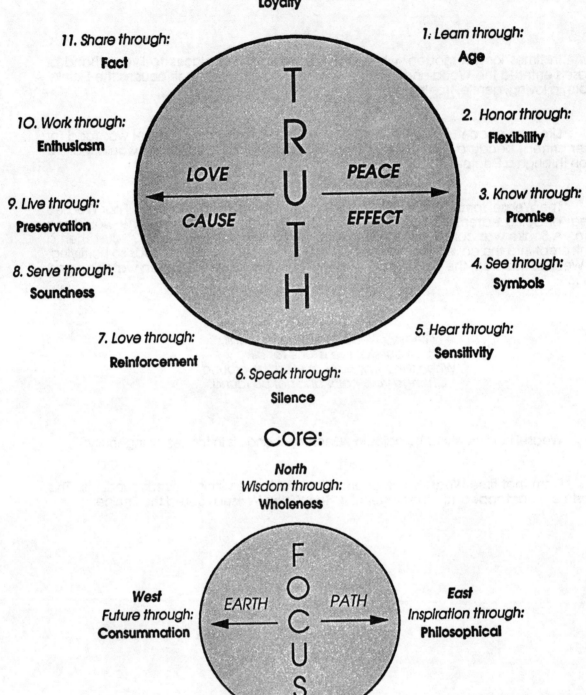

12. *Thank through:*
Loyalty

11. *Share through:*
Fact

1. *Learn through:*
Age

10. *Work through:*
Enthusiasm

2. *Honor through:*
Flexibility

LOVE   T R U T H   *PEACE*

CAUSE   *EFFECT*

9. *Live through:*
Preservation

3. *Know through:*
Promise

8. *Serve through:*
Soundness

4. *See through:*
Symbols

7. *Love through:*
Reinforcement

5. *Hear through:*
Sensitivity

6. *Speak through:*
Silence

Core:

North
Wisdom through:
Wholeness

West
Future through:
Consummation

F O C U S

EARTH   *PATH*

East
Inspiration through:
Philosophical

South
Lessons through:
Endurance

Whale

Decree of the Historian

When the Earth was quite young, many Water Creatures preferred to remain in the water rather than move onto the land. Whale was one of these Creatures. However, a young Whale wanted to experience an out of the water life.

He found an out of the way exit from the water where canals entered rocky shorelines or reefs. The young Whale discovered an Ancient Truth recorded in rocks in these natural canals. Because Water Creatures have a wide range to live in, the young Whale expressed that Whales were Ancient Ancestors. Whales have detectors that help to monitor what is happening to the Earth Mother.

When the young Whale returned to his Elders, he reported what he had seen along the underwater canals.

"Find someone who can follow your discovery," he was told.

It happened that when he returned, he made contact with a Two-Legged who understood Whale sounds. Much time was spent with this Two-Legged who swam with the Whale. When the tide was out, the Two-Legged was able to find symbols that recorded the movement of Earth energy on the rocks. As a result of this young Whale who wanted to walk on the Earth, we have learned that Animals and Birds can read thoughts by the sounds humankind emit. Animals and Birds can read body language. Plants hear sound and Earth energy. Some experiments have been conducted that bears out this discovery.

An Ancient tale by our People relates that a man discovered a Whale, that by chance, was trapped in one of these coastline channels. The man talked with the Whale while attempting to free him. The Whale had a scar from some other happening. The man, in time, was able to free the Whale, who immediately went out to sea. Every year, the man returned to the same place and always the same Whale returned for a happy reunion.

They romped together for several years. Then, on one of these reunions, it became apparent that the Whale wasn't going to keep his appointment. When the man was about to leave, the Whale limped in, gravely wounded by harpoons. The man stayed with him until he died. It was then the man knew that Whales are the Ancient Ancestors of the sea and kept the historical records of the Motherearth.

Da Nahol

Wolf
Contribution -Gratitude

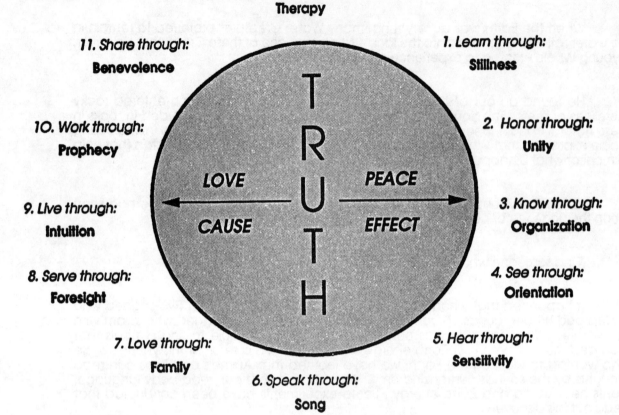

12. *Thank through:*
Therapy

11. *Share through:*
Benevolence

1. *Learn through:*
Stillness

10. *Work through:*
Prophecy

2. *Honor through:*
Unity

LOVE   PEACE

9. *Live through:*
Intuition

CAUSE   EFFECT

3. *Know through:*
Organization

8. *Serve through:*
Foresight

4. *See through:*
Orientation

7. *Love through:*
Family

5. *Hear through:*
Sensitivity

6. *Speak through:*
Song

Core:

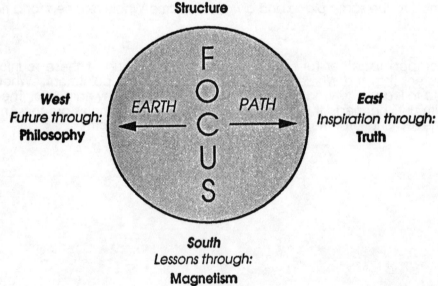

North
Wisdom through:
Structure

West
Future through:
Philosophy

EARTH   PATH

East
Inspiration through:
Truth

South
Lessons through:
Magnetism

Wolf
Decree of Gratitude

Many suns had come and gone,
Before Wolf dreamed of his decree.
A voice entered his sleep state,
That filled his heart with glee.

Thanksgiving forms the framework
To support the Sacred Quest
Each dream reveals its earthwork
While sleeping creatures rest.

Abundance quickens now
Stored in each body part
Instinct tells the way how,
Sleep heals the tired heart.

The Wolf Decree brings harmony
Where rest is common place
Thanksgiving dreams shall always be
To heal with each embrace.

The dream had spoken!

When the Wolf awakened, his heart was filled with joy. He crept from his earth den into a glorious day. The sun beamed loving rays upon his back as excitement sparkled his eyes.

Presently, Mouse happened by and Wolf gave chase to satisfy his morning hunger. They came to a giant rock where mouse climbed with ease. Wolf followed but lost his footing and plummeted to the ground his body painfully hurt. Wolf laid for days while Grandfather brushed his pitiful body with warm, soothing rays.

'Awaken,' said Grandfather Sun,
Your work has just begun.
Learn the Wisdom of rest,
Awaken, my friend life has no end --
Love lives within your breast.

Wolf stood and faced Grandfather Sun with the words still singing in his ears. "My body was healed!" he thought as he stretched after his long sleep. Presently Wolf realized what happened. He had received the Wolf Decree. Hurriedly he returned to his pack and spoke before the Council of Wolves.

I sing my song of Thanksgiving,
For the lessons, learned through dreaming.
Our bodies heal the best,
When restored through rest.

From that time Wolves dream of their Thanksgiving gifts and have passed on this knowledge of rest to heal the physical body. Today, Dogs, the descendants of Wolves, are often dreaming while their bodies are at rest.

Da Naho!

NOTES

NOTES

NOTES

NOTES

NOTES